Changing the Future
Redprint for Education

Changing the Future

Redprint for Education

The Hillcole Group

edited by
Clyde Chitty

the Tufnell Press

the Tufnell Press,
47 Dalmeny Road,
London, N7 0DY

First published 1991

British Library Cataloguing in Publication Data
A catalogue record for this book is
available from the British Library

ISBN 1-872767-25-7

Printed in England by Da Costa Print, London

Contents

Hillcole Papers available from the **Tufnell Press**,

Equal Opportunities in the new ERA
Ann Marie Davies, Janet Holland and Rehana Minhas
ISBN 1 872767 00 1

Something old, something new, something borrowed, something blue: Schooling, teacher education and the radical right in Britain and the USA
Dave Hill
ISBN 1 872767 05 2

Training turns to enterprise: Vocational education in the market place
Pat Ainley
ISBN 1 872767 10 9

Markets, morality and equality in education
Stephen Ball
ISBN 1 872767 15 X

What's left in teacher education: Teacher education, the radical left and policy proposals
Dave Hill
ISBN 1 872767 20 6

Foreword

This book has been written by the Hillcole Group. While most of the chapters have been written by individual members, or by small sub-groups, of the Hillcole Group, the book nevertheless represents a collaborative perspective. Each chapter has been discussed fully at one or other of ten Hillcole Group meetings held over the past year; and the writers of each chapter have developed and amended their analysis as a result of this systematic group discussion. The collection has been edited by Clyde Chitty to whom particular thanks are due for the final form in which the book now appears.

This book is Redprint One. It will be followed by others in an attempt to develop a coherent democratic socialist alternative to the current Radical Right and Centrist perspectives on education.

The Hillcole Group at the time of writing Redprint One are:

Pat Ainley
Stephen Ball
Caroline Benn
Clyde Chitty
Mike Cole
John Clay
Andy Green
Dave Hill
Janet Holland
Tamara Jakubowska
Ken Jones
Rehana Minhas
Gaby Weiner

Chapter One

General Principles for a Socialist Agenda in Education for
the 1990s and into the 21st Century

John Clay and Mike Cole

Before attempting to map out the agenda for a socialist education policy
for the 1990s and beyond, we have to take stock of the system as it exists
at present. This does mean that we have to acknowledge the influence
that Thatcherism as an ideology has had and the way in which this
ideology has been put into practice by a succession of Conservative
governments since 1979. The Thatcherite legacy that we have been left
with has been that of unashamedly introducing a hierarchy of systems
within education; whereby privileges in terms of money and status have
been poured in and conferred on the few whilst denying the majority
an equitable share of the resources. This has meant funding selective
initiatives such as the Technical and Vocational Education Initiative
(TVEI) generously, to re-orientate education for the world of work. The
Tories argued that schools were producing pupils who were anti-
entrepreneurial and anti-industry. To make this point even more
forcibly, the introduction of the TVEI programme into schools was
placed under the aegis of the Manpower Services Commission, an
offshoot of the Department of Employment. The clear intention at the
onset of the Programme was to target a selected number of schools in
LEAs across England and Wales.

The earliest attempt to break up the fragile consensus of the post-war
years was to halt the programme of comprehensivization of schools. The
1980 Education Act provided the 'Assisted Places Scheme' for pupils to
transfer from state schools to the private sector on a subsidized basis,
under the banner of 'parental choice'. The fact that this notional choice
was available only to the few and mainly benefited the already

privileged middle classes largely went unchallenged. The requirement for all schools to publish their examination results and the right of parents to appeal against the LEAs' school allocation for their children, along with the right to send them across LEA boundaries, undermined the principle of community provision and absolved parents as ratepayers from taking an interest in their own local educational provision. These rights were enacted for the sake of the few but their rhetorical impact was considerable. To argue that these new freedoms for the few were at the expense of enhanced quality provision for all by the consequent diminishing of centralized provision and planning, was seen as arguing against the right of parents to choose. In addition, the effect of the 1980 Act was for the system for the first time to be opened up to the idea of parents as *consumers* rather than as providers in a partnership with the community as a whole.

It could be argued that although Thatcher herself did not personally play a central role in radicalizing education, Thatcherism provided the economic and political context for the New Right to operate in and gave the ideological support which assured its ascendancy in education policy making. The authors of the series of Black Papers on education in the late 1960s and 1970s who criticized the abolition of the grammar schools and of the selection process at the age of 11 were finding themselves in a position to influence government policy directly. The Centre for Policy Studies, the Adam Smith Institute and the Hillgate Group are the natural heirs to that tradition, although it is important to emphasize that they have abandoned the defensive position of the early Black Papers in favour of policies designed to reconstruct the whole education system. The New Right are not a homogeneous bunch; and two distinct strands within this broad alignment are discernible. The ones who influenced the drafting of the 1980 Education Act and, more importantly, the 1988 Education Act are those who can be loosely defined as the free-marketeers. They see the main purpose of the education system as that of producing labour hierarchies for driving the capitalist economy. The 1986 Education Act was brought on to the statute book for a different purpose. This was influenced by the tendency within the New Right that Ken Jones labels the 'cultural restorationists' and Clyde Chitty calls the 'neo-conservatives.'[1] This group of academics and intellectuals expound a philosophy that is culturally supremacist and anti-egalitarian. They see their role as rescuing 'British Culture' from its diminution by 'alien cultures'. The adoption of equal opportunities policies, the promotion of multi-culturalism and anti-racism, and the attempts to make schooling more relevant to working class pupils are seen as undermining the traditional values and hierarchical structures that have kept the Right in power.

In this context we can see that the 1986 Education Act did not directly further the cause of bringing market forces to bear on the public sector of education but did nevertheless bring to the statute book several pet concerns of the New Right. These included the proscription of partisan teaching about political matters, school governors' control over sex education and the codification of police influence on schools - headteachers had to have regard to police representation about curriculum matters. Its aim was to restrain at local level the work of 'progressive' schools. These were schools that were seen as teaching all those concerns that were anathema to the 'cultural restorationists'.

The most far-reaching and controversial changes have been brought about with the passing of the 1988 Education 'Reform' Act. The National Curriculum can be seen as the brainchild of the 'neo-conservative' element within the New Right but the other major provisions are instrumental in moving us towards a fully market orientated system of public sector education. Its introduction by Kenneth Baker was preceded by his now famous announcement to the 1987 Tory Party Conference that 'the pursuit of egalitarianism [in education] is over'.[2] The provisions within the Act allow secondary schools and, more recently, primary schools of all sizes to 'opt out' of LEA control. This will have the effect of initially undermining and finally destroying educational provision that is collectively provided to meet local needs within a community through national and local taxation. Moreover, schools that 'opt out' are directly funded from central government and have no obligation to use the community-based LEA provision and services such as advisory staff and EWOs.[3] Thus the provision of pooled services for the remaining schools will inevitably deteriorate since poll tax capping prevents the community from increasing its resources to make up for the deficit through higher taxation. So far schools that have gained grant-maintained status have been those faced with closure through falling rolls or others that have sought to maintain selective intakes or that have held on to their cherished sixth form provision in the light of the threats of LEA post-16 reorganization.[4]

The 1988 Act includes proposals for open enrolment whereby secondary schools that are popular are obliged to increase their numbers up to at least the school's 'standard number', defined by 1979 'peak of the bulge' admissions. This was intended to introduce the notion of competition between schools in vying for pupils and thus force less popular schools to sharpen up their marketing skills or else 'wither on the vine.' However, the 'opt out' clause allows these vulnerable schools to seek Grant Maintained Status. The net effect is that LEAs are prevented from rationalizing school provision and planning strategically for the medium and long terms. The clear intention of this Government is to destroy LEAs. A right wing junior Minister for Education was quoted as saying to a conference organized by a pressure group that promotes the contracting out of public services to private firms, that local authorities were already becoming a mere postbox between central government and schools. He told the conference that the Government's reform had been planned to break up the monopoly of council schooling.[5]

The 'opt out' and open enrolment clauses in the 1988 Act are not designed to produce an effective and efficient system of education but are ideologically motivated and destructive in their effects on collective provision. The schools that have 'opted out' and sought grant-maintained status have been given up to £190,000 more for the year 1991/92. According to a report in *The Times Education Supplement* in March 1991, 41 of the original 49 Grant Maintained Schools were to benefit from this targeted largesse. All the schools involved get a basic budget equal to other LEA run schools but in addition get an extra 16 per cent to compensate for advisory and other central services provided by the LEA.[6] What makes these arrangements totally inequitable is that government guidelines to LEAs for the coming year ensure that LEAs retain no more than $7^{1}/_{2}$ per cent in their central budgets for the provision of central services. This way the majority of LEA schools will not only receive a less well-funded central LEA service but will in effect be subsidizing these 'opted out' schools; another case of robbing the poor to pay the rich. In terms of capital expenditure for repairs and new buildings, the story seems to be the same. Grant Maintained Schools have benefited to the tune of £326 per pupil compared to £83 per pupil spent in LEA maintained schools.[7] This highlights the need for us as Socialists to use the legislation in a way that promotes the social purposes of education as we see it.

The creation of CTCs has to be seen, within this context, as a crude attempt to bring market forces to bear and, as such, epitomises the neo-liberal attempt to shift from collective provision and collectivism to individualism and personal greed. CTCs tie the very small number of pupils who attend them directly to the market. CTCs, like private schools, are exempted from implementing the National Curriculum.

There are many clauses within the 1988 Education Act that will need to be repealed if we are to be able to pursue the kind of policies outlined later in this chapter. The fact that this Act locates so much direct power in the hands of the Secretary of State can be a two-edged sword. It does provide an incoming Socialist minister with the structures to effect change since the Act itself is remarkably unprescriptive.

A Socialist Agenda

The myth of 'parental choice' has to be exposed since this notion applies to only a minority of (middle and upper class) parents who can pay for such choice. A future Labour Government should provide meaningful choice through a truly comprehensive system, not only within the compulsory age range of 5 to 16, but for pre-school and post-16 education too. Education for life should be the immediate aim and on-going objective.

The social purposes of education need to regain primacy. The dichotomous divide between education and training should not be maintained and we must reject the premise that education is about producing labour hierarchies for the unfettered market economy.

In arguing for a repeal of the 1988 Act, we include in that an explicit rejection of the National Curriculum and seek to replace it with a curriculum that is underpinned by principles of equality *for all* and social justice. The curriculum has to be both enabling *and* empowering. We should therefore aim to redefine the curriculum content, away from its present form as a hierarchy of knowledge that assumes that learning occurs in a linear fashion. Its express purpose seems at present to be a mechanism for weeding out the vast majority and selecting the few who are chosen to proceed to the supposed cutting edge of new knowledge. We need to acknowledge that there is a difference between knowledge and skills required by all of us as 'literate citizens' and the different order of skills and in-depth knowledge required to pursue the study of a discipline to the frontiers. By this we mean that the knowledge and skills required for all citizens has to be of a much higher order and radically different in kind from the present; relevant to the needs of our global society in the next century. The development of 'collective intelligence' (Brundtland, 1987) that no longer relies on selecting the 'talented few' and labelling the rest as failures will enable pupils to flourish and avoid the present system of establishing a vast pool of 'trained incapacity'.[8]

We must argue for a change in thinking to take us beyond the 'welfare paternalism' and labourism of the post-war years and rather than merely advocating 'user involvement', we should propose a model of enabling 'self-advocacy.' In other words we must move away from thinking of the Welfare State as an inefficient centralized bureaucracy and move towards a model which not only *involves* the user but gives rights to and *empowers* that user. We should be concerned with more than merely having a voice in the provision of services which is then filtered, redefined and the final form determined by 'the professionals'. Self-advocacy is about our development as citizens, our understanding of civil rights and responsibilities and, more importantly, our ability to become active and articulate in the furtherance of these rights and responsibilities. It is about people making their own decisions about their own lives. To repossess the old socialist slogan hijacked but not implemented by the New Right - it is about power to the people.

One way of pursuing 'self-advocacy' is to extend the concept of the rights-based approach from benefit rights to welfare rights and social service provision. This 'bottom-up' democratic participation can be combined with 'top-down' guarantees of basic rights. Central services in education should be enshrined in law but delivered locally at community, neighbourhood, group and individual levels. This must be subject to continuous review and accountability. The process would ensure the development of an education service that is genuinely democratic at the local level. There is a need to move away from a system of citizenship based merely on duties to one based on rights and concomitant duties.[9]

A system of education that aims to fulfil the social, political and economic objectives we wish to see cannot be provided on the cheap. However, we must avoid using the jargon of the market such as 'value for money' since our values cannot be conveniently price tagged like a can of beans. We need to think of a new method and language that forms part of a larger social audit. We must argue that money being targeted to the already privileged and transferring resources inequitably to benefit the few at the expense of the rest may on paper appear to drive unit costs down but is fundamentally unjust.

Many educationalists on the Left have argued that 'new technologies' in a 'Post-Fordist' economy can be used to benefit the 'collective intelligence' and be truly empowering. Though this argument can possibly be sustained when considering the developed economies of the West, they take no account of the way in which denying access to technology has been a potent weapon in the maintenance of capitalist hegemony. Technology has also been used as the determinant of locating people into the hierarchy of any particular society.

What is Equality?

We currently try to define equality principally by highlighting existing inequalities arising out of differences in class, 'race', gender, sexual orientation, disability and age. As Radical Left Educators we need also to state the political, economic and social equality we seek in terms of outcomes and access.

Bryan S. Turner has distinguished three forms of equality, corresponding to different forms of citizenship existing at different levels and informed by a different politics. (See figure 1.)

Figure 1

Equality	Citizenship	Level	Politics
opportunity	legal	person	liberalism
condition	social	society	reformism
outcome	economic	production	socialism

In this diagrammatic representation, liberalism is a revolutionary movement to liberate what Turner describes as 'the person' from the fetters of legal restraint under feudalism. It gave rise, he suggests, to the notion of careers open to talent.[11] What liberalism really represents, we should argue, is the legal and deliberate liberation of white, able-bodied, heterosexual males and an accompanying *limited* social mobility for them. Reformism, in its turn, attempted to change the conditions of competition in capitalism by the legislative management of social conditions. Turner gives the example of free school meals as an illustration of reformism. Finally socialism attempts to bring about equality of outcome by changing what Socialists see as the real basis of inequality, namely the ownership and control of the productive basis of society.[12] Modern-day Socialists stress that equality of outcome should be a reality for all citizens and not just white, able-bodied, heterosexual men. Socialism does not, of course, abandon the principles of legal and social citizenship, but these will need to be amended often drastically to enhance the position of citizens currently excluded and/or discriminated against. There is an urgent need to extend access to those citizens currently experiencing denial or restrictions.

While believing that equality of outcome can be achieved only by changing the mode of production, as Socialists we also work towards more equality within the context of capitalist society. This has the dual benefit of alleviating hardship here and now and increasing the consciousness necessary for achieving more fundamental change. Such consciousness entails a vision of a society where competitive values are replaced by co-operative ones, where drudgery is either eliminated or shared, where the control of society is genuinely rather than formally democratic and where the organising principle is from each according to her/his ability to each according to her/his needs. As Democratic Socialists we would totally distance ourselves from Stalinist bureaucracy and lack of freedom and would embrace the concept of self-advocacy as outlined above. Self-advocacy is a powerful antidote to dictatorship and a vehicle for *advancing* freedom.[13] To reiterate, as Radical Left Educators, we take the need for long-term fundamental change as given but we are also concerned with short-term reform. In reforming the system in favour of those it exploits and oppresses (a worthwhile aim in itself) we aim also to open up the system so that it becomes a dynamic forum for a cooperative and democratic learning experience for all. In such a forum where *all* ideas and concepts are subject to critical scrutiny, we believe that socialist values will win the day. We aim not at propaganda or indoctrination (in fact we believe that the present system amounts to that) but at the creation of critically reflexive pupils/ students.[14] In our last section, we list some of the aims which we believe Socialists should continue to struggle for at all levels, which should become part of educational discourse and development and which we would encourage a future government to adopt.[15]

A Socialist Education Policy

The Aims of Education
We believe that the existing political, economic and ideological arrangements of society are such as to reinforce inequalities, to stifle creative potential, and to develop the personality in competitive ways. We believe that educational institutions increasingly reflect this wider system. Access to advanced education is still disproportionately denied to young women, and to black and working-class students. The content and the hidden curriculum of education leaves the majority of students with a deep sense of the unimportance of their own lives and with no conviction that knowledge can, in any broad sense, be really useful.

We believe that education, in and out of educational institutions, should concern:

The development of people's creative potential.

The development of students' understanding of the natural world, of the society in which they live, and of the work processes of that society.

The development of the capacity to work with others in controlling society's collective life.

Organization
We should introduce a new Pre-School System for young children that combines the learning function of nursery classes (DES based and disproportionately used by the middle class) with the caring function of day centres (DHSS funded, heavily used by working class parents). Integrating care and education throughout, the service should be available from the early months of life - for parents who want or need it, with flexible hours and varied venues, including care centres, schools,

playgroups, and child minders. Local authorities should be empowered to organize, set standards, help fund, equip and train for the service - using skills of local parents wherever possible.

The education system should be resourced so as to increase the educational opportunities for students who are disadvantaged, oppressed and under-represented in positions of power. Class size should be greatly reduced and staffing levels adequate to provide a wide range of teaching strategies, with support for special needs, ESL, curriculum development and implementation.

The present system of assessment introduced by the 1988 Education Reform Act should be abolished and exams should no longer serve as 'cut-off' points which restrict access to employment and further and higher education. At any time in their post-14 educational career, students should be able to accumulate credits for particular courses, which would build up to certificated qualification.

A unified system of fully comprehensive education should be created under local democratic control. The education of adults and school students should be integrated. All workers should have the right to educational sabbaticals and educational institutions should have the resources to provide for them.

The Curriculum

The curriculum should be made relevant to the majority of school students, should give an accurate picture of social reality and should be capable of engaging their interests.

Wherever appropriate, learning should be activity based and organized around student enquiry. The community should be used as an educational resource, and as material for critical investigation. The curriculum should encompass areas of knowledge such as philosophy, psychology, economics and sociology which are essential to understanding contemporary society.

The curriculum should be attentive to the real cultures of the people who live in Britain. It should not transmit the versions of the national culture promoted by the dominant class in society but should attempt to liberate students from oppressions. The culture which students bring to the school - including community languages - should be neither disregarded nor patronized and, *provided there are the resources* (not last of which must be substantial numbers of staff from black and other ethnic minority communities), culture should be at the centre of many aspects of the curriculum. At the same time, schools should aim to develop in all students the conceptual and linguistic advantages that the dominant group has long enjoyed.

Educational institutions should consciously organize to develop an internationalist, not an anglo-centric curriculum, and to challenge the racism, sexism, heterosexism and disablism which affect many students.

These measures would raise the levels of achievement of the majority of the school population and create the basis for a different attitude to learning. Whereas its basic outline would be the outcome of a national process of decision-making, every encouragement would be given to local initiatives to devise curricula and teaching methods that take up the general themes.

Democracy

Educational institutions should be centres of initiative, responsive to the communities in which they are placed. Democracy should be fundamental to their ethos and their functioning. We need measures to increase democracy and collective participation in the work of the institutions and in the planning of education policy. These would include:

Democracy among teaching staff with curriculum and associated decisions made through collective discussion and not management dictation.

Meetings of all who work in educational institutions to discuss matters of common interest and to break down professional barriers.

The promotion of trade unionism, through opposition to privatization, the restoration of school teachers' negotiating rights and the establishment of agreements that safeguard conditions of service.

Secondary, FE and HE students would have the right to organize and be consulted, and would be represented on an institution's governing body.

Local democratic control of educational institutions. Decisions about educational planning, resources and the broad framework of curriculum policy would be taken by education authorities which had been broadened to include representatives of community groups, parents and trade unions. Governing bodies, which should comprise LEA,

parent, teacher and student representatives, should oversee the
implementation of this policy at local level.

Education after sixteen
Our aim should be progressively to extend the comprehensive principle
upwards. To this end, local or regional authorities should be empowered
to create learning networks in existing schools, further and higher
education colleges, adult centres and workplaces, integrating them into
a universal and unified tertiary provision (ending the split between FE
and HE and the division between education and training). Each area
should have its own network with all adults given rights to use it. There
must be education and training allowances for 16 and 17 year olds,
grants for unemployed and retired adults, and paid educational leave
(PEL) for those at work - giving priority to those whom the education
system has failed to serve in the past.

This requires a great expansion of the system and the range of venues
where learning will take place, plus a dramatic increase in numbers and
types of access courses - so that no one is denied the first step on any
academic or vocational route. It means ending most of the YTS and JTS
and integrating only high-quality training with academic and vocational
education - with a nationally reorganized 'building block' system of
courses and credits (on the lines pioneered by the Open University).
This will vastly increase the choice and flexibility of learning programmes
available to adults - and reform the current 'jungle' of post-16 qualifications.
In time it will end the hierarchy of learning which segregates post-16
provision into three tiers: the academic (highly restricted and over
selective), the vocational (narrow courses starved of general educational
content), and the low-quality mass schemes providing few recognized
qualifications and little real skills training.

Increased funding would be reoriented to support courses, units,
programmes and research projects - rather than institutions, while
institutions themselves would diversify - to serve a larger range of
students. All centres of learning would relate more closely to their own
communities, including those with national and international intakes
and reputations.

There should be reforms of course content, extending the concept of
a broad and balanced education upwards from 16 to the adult years. The

commercialization of learning - with its narrowing courses 'bent' to serve short-term business interests at the expense of many other fields of learning - should be restricted, while other types of learning, including the humanities and general education, should be encouraged to expand.

Throughout, the equality of the educational and training experience should be monitored - to eliminate discrimination on the grounds of wealth, class, age, ethnicity, religion, sexual orientation, gender, disability, and level of previous attainment - and programmes of positive support encouraged.

Popular appeal

A socialist policy has great appeal: not just because it will devote more resources to education but because it will also ensure their fairer distribution. It will remove the selective barriers that restrict real choice, giving everyone meaningful rights - and community support - to advance themselves personally through education and training. Lastly, it will see that education develops away from a service giving priority to elites, small privileged groups, and short-term commercial interests - and renews itself as a community force designed to advance both individuals and society as a whole.

Notes

1. See Ken Jones, *Right Turn: The Conservative Revolution in Education,* London: Hutchinson Radius, 1989; and Clyde Chitty, *Towards a New Education System: the Victory of the New Right?* Lewes: Falmer Press, 1989.
2. Kenneth Baker, Speech to the Conservative Party Conference, 7 October 1987, London: Conservative Central Office.
3. In addition to 'opted out' schools and CTCs, there has been a rise in the private school population from 5.9 per cent of the total in 1980 to 7.3 per cent in 1989 and 7.4 per cent in 1990/91. However, as Hutton points out, that disguises the substantial growth in the privatized sixth-form population, estimated at nearly half in the South-west of England and at 39 per cent in London and the South-east. Although these figures are inflated by the exclusion of Further Education colleges, for which a regional breakdown is not readily available, as Hutton stresses, 'the message...remains stark'. Social apartheid is likely to intensify, he goes on, as the social composition of the university intake reflects the growing preponderance of qualified applicants from independent schools. Moreover,

new capital investment per head in private schools is five times higher than
in state schools. 'Not that anybody in the cabinet would give as much priority
to this [inequity] as, say, fighting for a new world order in Kuwait,' he
concludes, [since] they've chosen the inside track for them and theirs - and it's
that right to choose that comes first'. (W. Hutton, 'Why our choice -based
education system is developing into one of the world's most sophisticated
forms of social apartheid', The *Guardian*, 14 January 1991).

4. *The Times Education Supplement* 15 March 1991.
5. Ibid.
6. Ibid.
7. Ibid.
8. Brundtland Report, *Our Common Future, World Commission on Environment and Development*, Oxford: Oxford University Press, 1987.
9. S. Croft, and P. Beresford, 'User-Involvement, Citizenship and Social Policy', and P. Alcock, 'Why Citizenship and Welfare Rights Offer New Hope for New Welfare in Britain' in *Critical Social Policy*, Issue 26, Autumn, 1989.
10.   Turner, B.S. *Equality*, Chichester and London: Horwood Ellis Ltd and Tavistock, 1986, p.120.
11.   Ibid.
12.   Ibid.
13.   Here is not the place to counter the arguments which are levelled against socialism both from positions of privilege or principle and in terms of feasibility. For such a discussion see J. Baker, *Arguing for Equality*, London: Verso, 1987.
14.   Dave Hill, *What's Left in Teacher Education: Teacher Education, the Radical Left and Policy Proposals*, Hillcole Group Paper 6, London: the Tufnell Press, 1991; and Hill's chapter in this volume.
15.   The following is based on a list which was drawn up by the Socialist Teachers Alliance and Caroline Benn. It formed part of an article which appeared in *Interlink*, No. 8, June 1988.

Chapter Two

Critique of Alternative Policies

The Hillcole Group

Another term of Conservative Government would further increase centralization of control - combined with decentralization of responsibility for enforcing decisions. Financial policing would continue to go hand in hand with increasing prescriptive direction of curriculum and course development in schools and colleges. Governors, teachers, parents, students, lecturers and administrators at all levels would find their roles continuing to be limited to finding ways to cope with reduced expenditure, privatization, teacher shortage, and increased numbers of students. Their main task will continue to be geared to competition with each other at all levels - in short, less and less to do with educating; more and more to do with running educational 'businesses'. Policy at all levels - whether it is public testing or bidding for funds - would be designed to 'discipline' institutions into a hierarchy of obedient resource managers, cost cutters, and thought controllers - ready to sacrifice educational excellence, innovation, and equal opportunities in the pursuit of profit.

Yet a look at the education system - whether it be the state of buildings or the numbers proceeding to post-16 education - shows that such competition in the 1980s has lowered standards, not raised them; that a hierarchy of privilege inspires make-do and mend, the avoidance of innovation and the postponement of development. The goal becomes trying to stay afloat in a system deliberately designed to ensure that a continuing proportion of schools, colleges, users, professionals and courses go under or are replaced by 'profitable' courses, students and colleges. Democratic accountability will continue to decrease, while LEAs' powers to manage needs equitably will be progressively reduced and HMIs' independence increasingly compromised. In training, long-term national skills shortages will continue, while TECs divert training funds to favoured employers' short-term needs. Low-level mass training schemes for youth and adults will remain, expanding and contracting according to unemployment levels. Post-16 reorganization and development of qualifications will continue to be inadequate, underfunded and governed by criteria designed to preserve academic and social privilege. Equal opportunity policies at all levels of education and training will continue to be replaced by the new Tory 'blindness' to gender/race/class, ignoring deep structural inequalities affecting the working class, women, black people, older people and the disabled. Only the grossest discrimination will be tackled and then only by those with the means to use the costly legal system. At every stage differentiation will be stepped up, and privilege protected.

Possible New Conservative Development
And that's only the 'good' news. The bad news is that with Conservatives there is always the possibility of even wilder ultra-right policies being introduced - particularly as existing policies fail. For a hallmark of Conservative policy making has been to replace unfair, unpopular policy by policy even more unfair, unpopular and lacking in quality - as with successive training schemes in the 1980s. Among policies currently being promoted by Government ministers, MPs, and the tight little knot of interacting organizations which constitute the extreme right in education would be new laws to force schools to opt out (by requiring yearly balloting). This is part of the longer term goal of ending state education and forcing most schools into a hierarchy of 'private', self-perpetuating, government-funded trusts. Local authorities' powers would be further reduced (especially if their responsibility for funding education ended) - except for overseeing 'public' education for the underclass and policing the cuts. Schools accessible to working class areas would fall in number through a policy of mandatory school closures of 'unpopular' schools that 'cost too much', with pupils dispersed to schools in alien neighbourhoods. Meanwhile, selection would continue to be reintroduced, for once mass testing is underway, schools from the age of eight onwards would inevitably try (and be encouraged) to admit with reference to test scores. GCSE would be increasingly differentiated into 'grammar' and 'modern' papers[1]; 'A' level 'reformed' by differentiating

'high' and 'low' routes; and vocational education further divided. 'Core' education would be differentiated. Training would stay in the grip of local employers seeking to maximize short-term profits. Low level training schemes for older youths would be retained, with standards even lower, and compulsion remaining through threat of benefit withdrawal (if not new legal sanctions). Pupils would be encouraged to leave full time education at 14[2] with education ostensibly provided by employers, and additional funding going increasingly to employers rather than to schools or colleges. The 'voucher' system being introduced for training would be extended to schooling, perhaps at first through limited 'experiments', eventually universal. Arrangements for employer-led education - through Compact-like arrangements - would extend to further and higher education colleges, student numbers increased without commensurate public funding, by increased reliance on business sponsorship for education in universities and colleges, with matching public money diverted from higher education institutions to employers. Pressure would continue on colleges to market their courses to business interests and to increase their quota of wealthy non-British students. Student loans would remain and fees would be introduced on top - full cost for all students if some Conservatives have their way.[3] Alternatively, fee competition between institutions would escalate, the more elite able to charge more and consequently getting richer, while the more egalitarian ones get poorer. The same for means-tested 'scholarship' provision for the few, most of whom would have to rely on employers. Business sponsorship could also be applied to provide teachers and lecturers in schools and colleges, ostensibly to relieve shortages - to enable 'the market' to better control education at all levels. The power of school governors who are parents, teachers, or representatives of the community would be curtailed and powers handed to headteachers.[4] Government direction of teachers and lecturers, of the curriculum and courses, would increase, as would teacher and lecturer appraisal - with encouragement for institutionally negotiated pay differentials, to discipline the system's operatives. Locally, Conservatives would continue to refuse responsibility for dealing with racism, sexism and homophobia and continue to cancel high-quality equality programmes[5] and possibly also, acting directly against academic courses which deal with anti-racism and anti-sexism[6]. Private education in 'public' schools, private vocational and training colleges, would have subsidies improved, and new 'private' schools would be encouraged by state funding - through the mechanism of voluntary aided and opt-out status, including for new CTCs. Existing public schools could also get 100 per cent taxpayer support by being permitted to 'opt in' to GM status.[7] Public money to fund 'gifted' children in private education would be given to LEAs. School differentiation - 'magnets', specialist schools for the academic - would continue to be forced on unwilling school systems by Conservative local authorities (as has happened in Wandsworth). Any increases in expenditure for education will be largely deployed in these directions, not in spreading money equitably to all schools. The result will be increasing inequalities in the system. More choice for the favoured, less for the many.

As the public education service slowly declines, new crises will inspire more destructive 'activity'. It will also lead to more 'passing of the buck' from government to local authorities, governors, teachers, parents, LEAs, students and college administrators. All problems will be the 'fault' of the local council or the school or the college or the child or the parent or the ethnic group or 'lefty' college lecturers and 'Marxist' teachers, or the 'political' content of the course or the politically-motivated local community - never of the Conservative Government.

Contradictions and Disagreements within Conservative Ranks
Although a fourth term of office would give Conservatives a chance to press for the directions cited above, the field is anything but clear. Not only do Conservative policies clash increasingly with their declared objectives - like wanting to double the university population while also insisting on retaining both the underfunding and the selective academic structures that prevent such an increase - but within their own ranks opposition is mounting. The British Association's and CBI's criticisms[8] were devastating comments by normally conservative voices on ten years of failed activity following the policies of political ministers like Baker and Young. A decade of spending billions on education and training 'reform' designed to serve the British employer and economy, and it turns out employers say they are suffering the most acute skills shortages in the western world, and an equally acute shortage of graduates in management. All that posturing about raising standards, and it turns out Britain's school standards are almost the lowest in the

whole industrial world. Not only in terms of numbers qualifying but also in terms of the ground they have been able to cover. Disagreements within the Party stand to increase while the extreme right continues the old Black Paper cry of 'More means worse' at the same time as Conservatives officially claim to want major expansion. There is already opposition to the Ultra Right within Conservative ranks. The Conservative Education Association has long been fighting a losing battle against hard right views (and receiving scant media attention). Many in the Association are based in local authorities and live in some sort of real world. They still believe in the role of local authorities in planning education. Many thus found CTCs 'irrelevant' (as did most industrialists); many were worried by the privatization of universities and the 'disastrous' decline in civil research.[9] Even the wider faithful have doubts: hence the 1990 Conservative conference resolutions that spoke of 'the manifest failure of the Baker reforms' or the think-tank report expressing disapproval of the 'great.. ..hostility' that so many Conservatives have shown to the policy of Grant Maintained Schools.[10]

Disagreements within the Ultra Right
With Mrs. Thatcher gone, this tension between right and ultra-right will grow. Conservatism will also be undermined from within by the significant disagreements within the extreme right itself. A large section of this right continues to live in the 'grammar school' past, campaigning against course work, in-school assessment by teachers, or any child-centred learning - all regarded as 'trendy' and 'lefty'- despite the fact that the majority of Conservatives and Conservative voters endorse these practices, and support their local comprehensive primary and secondary schools as well. The hard right also opposes many of the policies which Conservatives have introduced themselves - like the National Curriculum, which some see as wholly incompatible with Conservatives' avowed policy of leaving schools free to manage themselves through policies like LMS. Even more oppose such centrepieces of Conservative reform as the GCSE examination,[11] which they see as inspired by the 'egalitarian ideology of comprehensivization' or a plot by 'leftist educational orthodoxy'. The extreme right meets opposition - such as the manifest disapproval by parents and schools of the present testing process at 7 - by calls for more frequent testing, new 16-plus exams, more emphasis

on 'facts', a return to grammar, and opposition to any change in the narrow A level course.

All this imprisons Tories in the past. But perhaps the most significant rift comes from the ultra right's dislike of relevance and the skills of problem-solving, which are so beloved by the modern Conservative entrepreneur. The hard right dislikes the 'entrepreneurial culture being foisted on us'[12] and calls for higher academic hurdles for the few. There is a real rift between Conservatism's ultra elitism and crass commercialism, and it is growing.

Other rifts created by the hard right threaten many schools with wholly dead-end controversies. One is the attempt to stir up much sterile debate on reading methods within primary schools. Another comes from attempts to protect 'pure religion' along with 'pure learning' in education (in some areas seen as merely a cover for 'pure race'). These are ostensibly arguments about preserving children's 'Christian' education; but they include attempts to remove 'Christian' children from schools with non-Christian majorities. Now there are campaigns to oppose multi-faith worship.

Overkill

Much of this activity began in the witchcraft hunting campaigns originally directed against Labour. The hard right spent years - with media assistance - inventing policies that the 'left' was supposed to have introduced - particularly related to issues of equality. Labour councils were regularly said to be in the grip of 'loony left' ideas, although research has since shown that most of these 'policies' - like banning the singing of 'Ba Ba Black Sheep' - never existed in any Labour Authority.[13] One result of these scares, however, was the badly-drafted reactive Clause 28 (on teaching related to gay issues) in the 1988 Local Government Act. Another was the equally badly-drafted clauses on promoting Christian worship. Another result more generally was a spread of bad feeling against those who were not white, heterosexual, Christian, Conservative and British. In time, of course, the fire was turned on Conservative councils themselves - as in Berkshire, where the religious advisor (having devised a well respected multi-cultural programme for schools) was repeatedly attacked by the right. Now it is Conservative councils as well that have to deal with ultra right objections to the Conservative's 1988 Education Act.[14] But it is not only authorities, it is also schools individually. The leader of the 'Real' Education Campaign accused the governors of the Church of England's Bishop Holgate School, York, including by name Dr. John Habgood, the Archbishop of York, of being 'men of Marx rather than Men of God' because the school had decided that its pupils, even though mostly white, should study 'other cultures' and have an 'active commitment to redress racial inequality'.[15] At the heart of the problem is the destructive influence of the hard right, which claims that to notice race is to 'politicize' people; and that to oppose racism is 'basically marxist'.

But it does not stop there. The hard right also disapproves of study related to peace or to Third World issues. Their well-known theorists list among education's greatest enemies: the UN Association, Christian Aid, the Catholic fund for Overseas Development, Oxfam, the World Studies network, One World Trust, the Leverhulme Trust, and Development Education Centres, particularly the World Studies Training Centre at the University of York. Elitist theoretical writing underpins populist campaigning by using the same dubious debating 'devices' it used for local authorities, of denouncing policies which are nowhere advocated. It is argued that the Left believes pupils should substitute peace studies for mathematics in schools, or that teaching about the Third World means teaching 'overthrow by revolution' and never reform; or that third world studies are 'directed to the dismantling of authority'.[16] The concept of a north/south poverty divide - a view held across the political spectrum - is attacked as 'imaginary' and said to be the result of Left propaganda. The hard right's beliefs increasingly highlight the clash between the Conservatives' official views and their traditional prejudices.

As hard right supporters continued to infiltrate Conservative policy-making, the hunt went on. First, the ILEA was abolished; then it was Labour Town Halls that were attacked. Now it is all town halls, Conservative controlled as well, that are suspect. Spurred on by the hard right's attack on local authorities,[17] bit by bit all locally elected education authorities are being deprived of their capacities to assist local schools and colleges. Given another Conservative Government, educational institutions democratically accountable to the electorate will be all but phased out. Democracy itself is what is being hunted to extinction.

Freedom and Censorship

Another sad result of education's infection by the hard right over the last decade has been that whole areas of learning have been condemned, particularly in the humanities, social sciences and environmental studies. In higher education too, disciplines associated with critical enquiry like history, psychology, religion, and philosophy have been downgraded or have had their departments closed down. Business studies have often filled this vacuum, many such courses being of low quality. Much vocational education, too, has been stripped of its social reference and redirected to narrow, instrumental goals. In further education, for example, there has been a determined attempt to phase out General Studies, the traditional 'broadening' component of vocational education. Any discipline that promotes critical enquiry appears suspect; hence the far right's battle over history teaching in the National Curriculum,[18] complaining that 'new History' has hi-jacked the curriculum. Even English is suspect to the far right, and there are calls for further controls through the powers of the 1988 Education Act on the English syllabus - on the grounds that English can 'foster ideas.....associated with the left'.

Possibly the hard right comes to believe in the reality of its distorted world, which includes fear of the teaching and lecturing professions themselves, as well as of those who prepare people to be teachers. It wants the teaching profession patrolled to root out 'teachers.....influenced by marxism'.

To read the pamphlets of the far right is to enter the realm of the absurd, although it is dangerous to live in a deluded world they themselves invent in which the majority of teachers (traditionally, Conservative voters) are treated as subversives or at best as 'brain-washed'. Many teachers have now lost faith in the Conservative Government, but only the extreme right persists in thinking this is due to too much reading of the Communist Manifesto.

The far right speaks indiscriminately of marxists and terrorists as one and the same. Left-wing bias is found everywhere. The Southern Examination Board's religious syllabus was taken to task for using quotations from Bishop Tutu and Martin Luther King.[19] The same Board was attacked as 'left wing' because its social studies included a question on what a jobber did on the stock exchange and for a unit on discrimination faced by American blacks in the 1950s and 1960s. It was suggested that a more acceptable topic would be the contribution that the 'cadet corps' has made to youth in the UK.[19]

The ultimate danger from the hard right and its backers comes from the continual demands for regulation of thought within the education process. Increasingly, its 'reform' proposals are designed to exclude all but one point of view: their own. They promote ending of pluralism of opinion, succumbing to the very censorship they started out opposing. Under the banner of freedom they try to prevent the views of others from being heard. There must be only one right way of teaching about society, the economy, the nation or the world.

The danger posed by the ultra right lies in its power to 'hi-jack' the Conservative Party, and convince it that it is politically expedient to continue down paths which require the Government to ignore majority opinion in education on an increasingly wide range of issues. There is no sign at all that with Mrs. Thatcher's departure - or with the new Conservative face - that the hard right's destructive influence is any the less in education.

1991 Policy

Proof of this comes in the latest round of policy proposals on further education contained in the second of two documents, *Higher Education,* 1991, and *Education and Training for the 21st Century,* 1991. The main proposal of the first was to end the so-called 'binary' line between universities and polytechnics by having a common funding council and letting polytechnics award their own degrees. One motive was to expand numbers in higher education - not by extra funding but by 'competition' between institutions. What it really means is that numbers will increase with resources staying the same: expansion on the cheap. At exactly the same time a new binary line was created in the second policy document by taking further education colleges out of local democratic control and setting them up under an appointed national funding council - with regional advisory arms. 16-19 education will be cut in two. Post-18 education will be cut in two. Adult Education will be cut in two. Learning inside the FE colleges will be restricted according to government decree, for although they may run A level, GCSE, basic skills and access courses, they will shed their higher degree work and be restricted to developing vocational qualifications for employers. To this end, they will be run on competitive lines, overseen by 'strong industrial' and 'commercial' representation. There will be no accountability to any locally elected body and no guarantee that the local community's wider educational needs will be met. The policy was not developed for educational reasons but to remove expenditure from local authorities in order to lower the charge of the disastrous poll tax. The Government's only way out was to take it out on the education system.

Policy from a Range of National Campaigns and Interest Groups
Throughout the 1980s there was steady criticism of government policy. Many called attention to the damaging effects of cuts in funding or the lowering of standards after privatization of services. Others to the substitution of 'market forces' for educational criteria as the regulators of quality and efficiency which was turning education from a service into a commodity. Comment also focused on increasingly centralized control, the loss of democratic accountability and the reintroduction of divisions and inequalities at all levels.

Overshadowing them all in recent years has been criticism relating to Britain's failure to keep pace with other industrial countries in terms of percentages of the age group receiving education before the age of five and after the age of 16, including participating in higher education, and attaining high levels of technical skill. Whether these drawbacks are seen as Britain lagging in the international industrial race - or as a failure to develop human and social potential - depends on the political point of view. But common to all political perspectives is a sense of urgency about upgrading and expanding the British education and training systems.

1) Omnibus Groups

a) *The Council for Educational Advance* (CEA) is typical of an organization supported by a very wide range of opinion from the non-Conservative majority, limited to broad policy proposals that command wide support. Among these are a return to the practice of consultation of all users, and the 'ballot box' as the only accountability in education.

b) *The Educational Alliance* was another large group - made up of 34 trade unions, national organizations such as The British Youth Council and the WEA, and all the main teacher organizations: NAS/UWT, NUT, NATFHE, the AUT and Scotland's EIS. Now merging with the CEA, its alternative policy was a broad 'cradle to grave' programme, including a pre-school care and education service, publicly funded meals and milk in schools, a 'completely comprehensive' secondary system, 16-19 education for all with grants for those on full-time courses, a statutory system of training, more access to higher education and greater opportunities for continuing education. It also called for a reversal of cuts.

c) While umbrella organizations like the Alliance offer generalized policy, limited-objective organizations like *TANEA - Towards a New Education Act* - confine policy to a specific area. TANEA, a group of academics and educators concerned with change through national legislation, supports the establishment of a new council of 'all legitimate interests' in education, to give advice to the Secretary of State - as well as a new Education Act. The Act would incorporate 'the better part' of existing legislation but recast it to redraw the balance between national and local control of education (restoring the LEAs' role), and between competition and co-operation (strengthening the latter) - as well as providing for an overhaul of birth to five provision. Although limited largely to schools, TANEA's principles apply throughout education: 'justice is an attainable educational ideal'; and secondly, greater equality requires positive action involving 'varying provision' within the system.

2) Special Interest Groups

There are dozens, if not hundreds, of special campaigns occupying the centre leftwards, each restricted to policy-making in the area of its own interest -from teachers concerned about specific subject areas, women's groups concerned about gender disadvantage, to the disabled calling attention to their special needs. Each provides important guidance for general policy.

a) *The Campaign for Anti-Racist Education* (CARE) is one example. It urges acknowledgement of racial, gender and class inequalities in education, and proposes that these be monitored by law. Designed to assist racial and ethnic minorities, policy includes universal nursery and day care provision, the abolition of all academic selection, including streaming inside schools, as well as the abolition of the Government's proposed testing programme nationally. CARE also wants an end to required Christian worship in schools, substituting either multi-faith assemblies or secular ones (although while voluntary religious schools exist, all religions should have equal rights to set up schools). Under CARE's proposals, education would be returned to LEAs, LMS would be abolished and there would be universal access to higher education.

Critique
Any selection of campaigning groups from the range of 'progressive' policy-making campaigns shows quite a lot of consensus. All support the return of a proper public education service managed by democratically elected authorities. All support extending education to more people and new age groups while also ending present 'restrictive practices' like streaming or selection. Although many of the changes proposed would provide antidotes to some of the more poisonous aspects of Conservative policy, the means many advocate are revivals of practices of the past - like standing advisory councils and educational priority funding. We have to consider whether merely updating the principles of the 1944 Act - which is what many of the proposals from these groups amount to - really offers the kind of alternative that is adequate for the new century.

3) The Education Unions
Education unions have always been policy makers as well as bargaining organizations, and although their work in this respect is sporadic, it is usually influential.

   a) *The National Union of Teachers* (NUT) has been committed since 1969 to a fully comprehensive school system; and more recently, to ending assisted places, and bringing opted-out and CTC schools back in to local authority control. In the wake of the 1988 Act it examined the national curriculum,[20] where, starting from a critique of rigidity, over-control and under-resourcing, it advocates replacing it with 'areas of experience' and a new national consensus on the skills and 'core' of knowledge needed by each age group - with 'the majority of the content.....left to local negotiation between teachers and the community'. It opposes the Government's plans for national testing and wants teacher assessment - within national and local guidelines - to 'become the main means of assessing pupils'.

These proposals which assert the rights of teachers to more control of the education they teach, sharing this with parents and students, would mean developing education as increasingly teacher and community-led rather than government dictated. This has relevance to containing disadvantage as well as to preparing for an unknown future. The NUT believes education should be 'related to the sort of society we want to see', restoring to educational planning an important component which the last ten years - with the drive to detach education from any social context - has all but removed.

b) *The National Association of Teachers in Further and Higher Education* (NATFHE) has long had a rolling programme of policy proposals for education and training after 16. It includes a strong commitment to general education within vocational training, a comprehensively reorganized system, and a curriculum that unifies academic, vocational and training education. It envisages a large expansion of post-school programmes - with eventual equality of funding for all institutions - and, more recently, a commitment to comprehensive community colleges that incorporate adult and community education. Individual further education colleges, anxious to respond to local needs, take policy-making further. For example, one (Bilston College) advocates the immediate establishment of a partnership with the LEA, other colleges, schools, employers and outreach centres - to start a genuinely comprehensive reorganization of education and a unified delivery after 16.

c) *The Association of University Teachers* (AUT) - is one of the few educational unions to deal specifically with the problem of under-representation of the working class in education - and the need to develop policy that corrects this situation, particularly in higher education.[21] Recent publications[22] concentrate upon the 27 per cent deterioration in pay since 1979, advocating new pay machinery involving government directly (with an immediate 30 per cent salary increase),

additional staffing numbers, restoration of research funding, and attention
to a deteriorating infrastructure.

Critique

It is no longer a strength for unions to be so confined to specific sectors.
Their policy-making urgently requires co-ordination where sectoral
interests overlap. NATFHE and the NUT should have a joint working
party on policy relating to tertiary education and training - likewise also
NATFHE and the AUT. Perhaps even all three, if post-16 education is to
be seen as a coherent whole. Clearly also the unions representing pre-
school staff, both teaching and non-teaching, both social services and
education, need to plan together for any agreement about reorganization
of that sector to be successful. Joint working is also the only way major
issues that straddle all age groups -like teaching ratios and funding
according to age - can be debated and agreed. So far there have been
few attempts to undertake this co-operative activity, and all governments
find it easy to play one union off against another when serious
reorganization begins in any of these areas. The failure of unions to
come together to try to agree new arrangements relating to mutually
desired pre-five or post-16 changes could seriously delay development
in these sectors. Similarly, any alternative policy for the Left should
include a requirement for unions' co-operative activity in the planning
process.

4) The TUC

Although individual unions have policy-making groups that touch on
both training and education, it is to the TUC that we look for an agreed
amalgam. In some areas the TUC is active in policy making, in others
curiously silent.

One area of activity has been the reform of under-fives' care and
education, starting in 1978 with *The Under-Fives Charter* and still
continuing.[23] Based on the needs of working people, particularly
women, TUC policy envisages far-reaching publicly-controlled
reorganization of nursery education and day care facilities into a single
new under-fives service. It would restructure DES and DSS provision to
provide in addition for the growth, development and professional
recognition of childminding, playgroups, workplace creches and 'out of
school' provision for older children. The TUC's latest proposals summarize

the social importance of early-years comprehensive reform for the parents and workers of any community, and ask for a new legal duty to be laid on elected Education Authorities to plan it.

Education and training for youth and adults is the other main area of TUC policy concentration. Its *Plan for Training*, 1984, set out joint TUC/ Labour Party policy. It was based on support for the MSC's Task Group Report of 1982, which backed clear post-16 divisions between vocational apprenticeships, full-time academic education, and a 'recast' version of the Government's YTS. It also accepted that training should be divided from academic education, and had little to say about the latter or about training for the professions. Throughout the 1980s, both the Labour Party and the TUC supported the Government's current training schemes - including all versions of YTS - maintaining only that Government policy 'distorted' what could be a good policy if run by Labour. *Plan for Training* suggested improvements for MSC policy like 'programme review teams' in workplaces and educational maintenance allowances for the low income trainee.

During the middle 1980s, as YTS became increasingly discredited, the TUC confined itself to criticism of the way it worked. Not until *Skills 2000*, 1989, did policy get overhauled. Here suggestions for change were general - for example a greater 'education element' in training. Competitive industry is seen as the driving force behind work-related and personal development, and this is reflected in policy for a system of 'credits' given to each young person - to pay for a course either in education, a training scheme or work. The NCVQ to devise a system of qualifications, where all would have the 'right to progress' to a recognized qualification and to have a Record of Achievement. While existing youth and adult training schemes continued, they would be voluntary, better paid, and more attention would be given to qualifications and jobs. Racial discrimination would be tackled by a legal change to the Race Relations Act. Those being trained at work would have TU pay rates for work periods. The delivery system remains the same as in 1984 except that the old programme review teams now become 'workplace training committees' - and there would be statutory rights for workers to be consulted through a 'plan' that each firm would draw up- spurred by a non-statutory training charter. TECs would remain, but expand their membership to include TU representatives. Sectional bodies would be recreated to oversee training planning, pinpoint needs and monitor progress, while a tripartite body 'along the lines of the MSC' would be recreated. (For more recent joint TUC/Labour Party policy, see under Labour Party.)

Critique

The TUC's 1984 *Plan* suffered from being neither a real critique of government policy nor a full set of alternative proposals. It also said nothing about creating jobs.

Although *Skills 2000* added substantial improvements in the conditions and pay of trainees on schemes, postulated greater expenditure on training and claimed to want a more unified system, its proposals envisaged training and education as largely separated. Although there was support for an upgraded vocational education and training through a 'credit' system (in part upstaged by government 'vouchers') and proposals that mitigated many of the harsh conditions imposed by Conservatives, there was still tacit support for a divided system of academic and vocational education. In short, it is mainly training for 'working-class' work that occupies TUC policy making. Academic education and professional training figure little. This inevitably further underlines a traditional divided approach. A second general criticism is that much policy (including that agreed jointly with Labour) is a straight recreation of the tripartite past - when government, employers and unions supposedly agree on how things should be run and pass this down the line. There is also educational policy from the past - like the commitment to develop HE on the Robbins principle. There is some naivety about the capacity of individual young people to choose the education or training they want when that 'choice' will be so heavily dependent on employers' selectivity, employers' policies of day release and employers' willingness to pay for training. There is also some scaling down of earlier demands, missing for example was the earlier legal requirement on all employers to release 16-18 year olds for E and T. Paid Educational Leave is now 'long term'; previously it was to be 'negotiated now'. The TUC understandably wants to convince the public that the nation can 'afford' its programme, but the proposed structures for delivery contain few suggestions for democratic accountability either locally or regionally, nor much encouragement for decision-making at local levels - all of which would seem to be urgently required.

The Political Parties

1) Liberals, SDP and Liberal Democrats
During the 1980s (before they formed part of the SLD) the Liberals criticized the Government from an individualistic perspective, proposing a Department of Education and Training, a 'post-school credit system', more 'participative' education, LEAs that issued reports on equal opportunities - particularly gender - and traineeships without compulsion for everyone between 16-19.

Before it merged, the SDP in 1986 published an important consultative paper suggesting that a billion extra each year (minimum £700m) would be needed to pay for the expansion required in education - for example free part-time degrees (it also favoured the addition of two year degree courses). In the same year *Tertiary Education for All* proposed full-time academic or vocational education with a 'through period of 14-18 made up of modules and credits'; means-tested basic benefit grants (for about a third of the 16-19 age group); a new national body - alongside existing boards - to cross credit existing exams and qualifications; a requirement that LEAs keep track of 16 and 17 year olds; the International Baccalauréat to replace A levels; and at 16-plus, 'assessment of measurable competence in a broad range of skills.' It would also 're-examine' whether it was necessary to have external exams at all at 16-plus. It would 'review' independent education and Oxbridge entry to get fairer systems; and require employers to release 16 and 17 year olds two days a week or provide education and training themselves to approved standards. The organization of the system would be a mix of tertiary colleges and sixth forms, with local areas left to choose.

2)Liberal Democrats, 1990
The SLD retains the old Liberal mix of education as 'quality of life, self fulfilment, and competitive success' in its own policy.[24] Earlier commitments are merged and new ones added, in particular a pre-school entitlement from 3-5, with LEAs drawing up plans giving more financial weighting to ages 4 to 7; and the re-absorption of CTCs and GM

schools. The National Curriculum Council would stay - to provide a national framework - but schools would be given more chance to produce their own versions. Sex education would be required to be included. LMS stays too but each school would have an annual negotiation with the LEA about its needs, using concept of 'average teacher costs'. Attainment targets would go - with teachers undertaking diagnostic testing themselves, starting with universal testing in reception classes. There would be a General Teaching Council - but pay bargaining would also be at local level. 25 per cent of places on governing bodies would go to teachers. Private schools would be kept but charitable status reviewed. No further religious schools would be created and existing voluntary schools would be encouraged to become 'state maintained'. There would be a Special Needs Service in all LEAs, and some equalization of expenditure on buildings between schools.

Proposals after 16 update the earlier SDP and Liberal policies with some additions like crash courses to meet skills shortages. There would be a two day minimum education for all those in employment up to 18. After 18 the binary line would be ended and a Higher Educational Council created. Three-year degree courses would be reformed into a combination of two year diplomas, three year bachelor and four year masters degrees - with encouragement to reorganize all courses on modules and credits. All HE colleges would be empowered to grant their own awards. Funding 'would follow students', the Government paying the costs of the course to the institutions chosen. Non-means tested grants for HE could also be extended to FE. In training, TECs would be abolished and the LEA and employer would meet training needs, each LEA required to submit a plan after consulting unions and employers. Creches and distance learning would be attached to all post-16 institutions.

Critique

These changes would free and extend the system considerably, particularly higher education. SLD reforms are almost entirely education-led and the plans for change to a modular/credit system from 14-plus through higher education, follow an American pattern.

But SLD plans also retain a great many *laissez-faire* Conservative policies, including open enrolment with its hidden selective bias against an equitable system of schooling. There is no commitment to end selection. There is thus a disparity between its commitment to full comprehensive education and its plans for competition between institutions at all levels, including for funding. There is a similar disparity between commitment to curricular and assessment reform after 16 but none to institutional reform beyond saying the system would become 'coherent'. Sixth forms will remain, pitted against tertiary colleges. Apart from day release before 18, plans for training at any age are very sketchy. The unions' role is minimal and employers are clearly in the saddle all the way. Overall (except for one proposal on school building) there is an ominous absence of commitments to equality or redistribution of resources - despite the up-front acceptance that taxes might have to be raised to pay for education's development.

3) The Green Party

Green policy on education is set out in two short sheets and a longer Manifesto.[25] Inevitably these criticise education's limited approach to the environment (e.g. inserting nature-watch slots in an unchanged curriculum) and argue for 'improving education's role' in relation to our ability to live 'in harmony with the biosphere'. But Greens also mount a critique of the education system as a whole, finding all certification and examinations socially and financially wasteful. They would phase them all out. The National Curriculum and mass testing would also be ended. Government control would be restricted to ensuring schools provide adequate literacy and numeracy education, while the rest of the curriculum would be devised by schools individually.

Ideally, school work would be project-based and co-operative - and competition would be phased out. Schools would be mixed sex, and, if possible, run without hierarchical structures. They should be small (although universities could be large). Universities would serve local communities more; and degrees would be phased out (and replaced by 'descriptive diplomas'). Research would have to be vetted as 'socially valid' before being granted funding.

A reorganized system would end education's wasteful 'bureaucracy' - with decisions made (and schools run) entirely locally, possibly at 'parish' level. The LEAs' function would be restricted to running centres where scarce courses and equipment could be made available, innovation encouraged, and an ombudsman provided.

Selection would be ended, including in public schools (which would have to admit pupils, regardless of parents' ability to pay). Religious schools would be retained. There would be neighbourhood schooling - with a strong community education remit - for those who do not 'self-select' to private or religious schools, or to the non-community new schools which groups (including green groups) might possibly set up. More teachers would be made available. Further and higher education would be available for 'all who want it'.

Critique
The Greens are the only political party with proposals that give education a completely social purpose: to 'harness the caring capacity latent in all individuals'. They are the only party to commit education to ending discrimination against gay people. They are also the only party whose intention is to 'change the whole emphasis' of education and attempt a radical reform by shutting down most current practice. They go so far that they almost merge with the libertarian ultra-right: 'schools would have almost complete freedom to go their own way'. And no schools could be closed if there were any objections. There would also be part-time education (on a voluntary basis) for both ages 5-7 and the over-14s, leaving, in effect, only six years of compulsory schooling.

Policy is minimal and generally 'back of an envelope' in development, possibly only a personal view. It has Illich-like features in its rejection of certification, but unlike de-schooling, does not link education to improvements in the social and economic circumstances of groups and communities. It is countryside based, and middle-class in orientation - and has no apparent appreciation of any inequalities within the system. There is nothing on equal opportunities, disadvantage or the inner cities. Policy also has nothing on training or vocational education. It is university oriented with little or nothing on adult education or FE. Throughout there are serious contradictions: e.g. to extend education while reducing entitlement; to develop locally based schools while encouraging non-locally based schools; summed up in its overall commitment to many sweeping changes while also committing itself to preserve 'tradition' and to make no 'sweeping.. ..changes.'

4) *The Nationalist Parties*

a) *The Scottish Nationalist Party's* policy documents[26] include a nationally overseen curriculum locally administered, giving opted out and CTC schools five years to return to LEAs or go independent, and developing multi-cultural education in all schools. Foreign languages would start at infant stage, and there would be a big increase in Gaelic-medium teaching. The SNP is committed to comprehensive community schooling, with a common course system in the earlier years and common leaving dates. All higher education would be administered from Scotland and students would get grants rather than loans, including at 16-plus. YTS would be abolished and replaced by a national 'apprenticeship scheme' on the German model.

Critique

SNP policy combines liberal and labour elements, but its main thrust is the transfer of control to Scotland, together with stepped-up European links. The 'system', however, would stay much the same, and little fundamental reform is contemplated.

b) *Plaid Cymru*

The Welsh Nationalists' policy[27] like the SNP - emphasises transfer of educational management to Wales through creation of a Welsh Curriculum Council and a Welsh Examinations and Assessment Council, together with transfer of higher education to the Welsh Office. Welsh would be a core subject of the curriculum for everyone. The National Curriculum, however, is seen as 'state indoctrination' and would be modified. Testing would also be more flexible and come under the control of schools individually. There is commitment to a fully comprehensive system, including the retention of small schools where required.

Critique

Though radical in intent and willing to pioneer a new path for the curriculum and assessment, on reorganization there is little forward thinking. Issues relating to 16-19 course reform, assessment, and institutional reorganization are completely side-stepped, and there is very little on training beyond general support for 'Welsh people trained for Welsh posts'.

5) Smaller Socialist Groups

a) *The Communist Party* is currently considering its future and has no up-dated policy available. There is nothing recent on further, higher or pre-school education; and no overall perspective on the system as a whole.

The now defunct YCL (1987), however, advocated a unified and modular training system for youth, a voice for school students, grants for all full-time students after 16, resistance to TVEI, and training schemes only with union approval. Earlier the Party published *Defend Comprehensive Schools* (1986), which advocated neighbourhood, non-selective schooling, abolition of streaming and setting, opposition to GCSE and CPVE and support for a genuinely common examination. It proposed a reformed A level on the lines of Scotland's Action Plan.

b) *The Independent Labour Party* (ILP) consistently opposed all youth training schemes, including YTS, and argued for an integrated education and training system for everyone.

c) Several individual unions have also pursued this line, and in 1987 these forces joined together to produce the seven volume report of education and training, the *National Labour Movement Inquiry*.[28] It contained a long list of positive proposals for unifying education and training, and many more related to equalizing opportunities in education and training for working class young people, women, gays and lesbians, black and ethnic minorities, and the disabled. A third set related to democratic accountability.

d) The education working group of *The Socialist Movement*, a non-sectarian cross-section of socialists published *Education: Towards a Socialist Perspective* in 1990. It cites failures in the progressive policies of the 1960s and 1970s and suggests an alternative built on struggles to defend education as a public service. Policy is set out sector by sector, and includes dismantling or replacing the National Curriculum, mass testing, LMS, open enrolment, and 'formula funding'. It supports educational self-organization that empowers groups as well as individuals.

6) Smaller Socialist Parties

Although the smaller socialist parties comment on education from time to time - and several have mounted very effective campaigns against the Government on individual issues like privatization or the exploitation of youth on training schemes - the main thrust of their educational activity is on industrial issues (like redundancies, pay, and negotiating rights) or on funding to the system. Their criticism is directed against the Labour Party as well as the Government, with Labour's Policy Review summed up by one as follows.[29]

'It represents Labour leaders eager to get their hands on the reins of office.. ...Instead of labour gradually changing capitalism it is capitalism that has gradually changed the Labour Party'.

Critique

In Communist papers there was a fundamental split between policy for education (entirely school based) and policy for training and youth (largely college and workplace based). In the ILP and NLM *Inquiry* extensive policy proposals for ages 16-25 are unintegrated with other years. The Socialist Movement's positive policy proposals are less well developed than its negative critique. The criticisms of the smaller socialist parties are often stringent - and some of their campaigns effective, particularly locally - but their contribution to policy development is limited.

7) The Labour Party

Labour went into the 1980s with an education and training policy passed at all levels - as part of a rolling policy programme that had continued from the 1970s. In 1982 Conference passed the latest version and the Party published a 16-19 document outlining the next stage of the comprehensive reform (*Learning for Life*, 1982). During the following five years, however, work on up-dating policy lapsed, with Party activity increasingly directed to 'answering' Conservative legislation - in effect, 'reacting' critically rather than preparing an alternative. Typical policy papers at the time were the series of charters - generalized, short documents with little that was new, stressing areas Conservatives had highlighted - like 'choice' and 'standards'. They seemed designed to show Labour could outdo the Tories on their own ground. Meanwhile, promised policy details of Labour's own 14-18 curriculum and assessment plans failed to appear year after year. Only when the SDP produced its own tertiary proposals in 1986 was Labour spurred to bring out a short paper. It followed SDP lines closely and was markedly less detailed than its 1982 document.

On training matters, Labour held firm to the MSC and all its works, and, along with the TUC, supported YTS and adult training schemes through their various manifestations. Criticism was directed to attacking the Government for failing to fulfill the schemes' potential. Locally, different Labour authorities (where they were also managing agents) had different training policies. No attempt was made to agree on a national line. There was disagreement between front bench spokespersons about crucial features of future policy - for example whether a Labour government would require industry by law to contribute financially to training. In a single week in 1986 two frontbench spokespersons gave completely opposing commitments, John Prescott said there would be a requirement, Roy Hattersley said there would not. Other frontbench spokespersons convened working parties and produced papers (*Options for Labour*, 1986, was an example, prepared by the spokesperson for training) criticizing Government education and training policy and outlining alternative options, but recommending none.

a) *Labour Conference Policy.* If national policy-making had become sporadic and ill-defined, there was policy continuity, as always, through the Labour Party Conference - important because its views have a way of prevailing in the long run. At the very least, successful conference resolutions indicate the pressures any Labour Government would be under.

The continuation of comprehensive education reform - with an end to all academic selection - topped the list of successful resolutions year after year during the 1970s and 1980s. Significantly, these extended comprehensive reorganization to cover pre-school, post-school and post-18 education. Resolutions on training, highly critical of the MSC and

Government schemes, were also regularly passed. As early as 1986 Conference voted to abolish YTS.

With policy concentrated on post-16 development, there were calls for 'the reorganization of all education and training in a unified and universal education service after 16' (1985) - as well as for a new Education Act (1986) to provide a democratic, comprehensive, locally based education service for all ages, free at point of use and subject to nationally agreed minimum standards relating to staffing, capitation and buildings (1986). The Act should also eliminate sexism and racism; and provide a statutory right for everyone to continue education full or part-time. It should include the 'planned public ownership of the private school system', an end to the binary line after 18, and statutory rights to education for all adults. As well as full financial support for students and trainees after 16.

From 1988, Conference policy increasingly concentrated on reversing Conservative changes, particularly the 1988 Act. Among 'reversals' passed in 1989 were an end to YTS and the Job Training Scheme; an end to open enrolment in schools; the return of GM and CTC schools to local authority control; the abolition of compulsory tendering and the return of services to LEA control; the replacement of the National Curriculum by a common core under national guidelines; an end to compulsory national testing; and an end to student loans.

In 1990 Conference passed a renewed call for an Education Act from Labour, including abolition of the present LMS arrangements, and introduction of national regulations for class sizes and non-contract teachers' time. The training resolutions passed included the right to paid release from work up to 18 for vocational training. Defeated was a long resolution that contained a call for the state education system to be developed in a fully secular direction.

b) *The Education Forum*. During the early 1980s Labour abolished its extensive network of education policy committees - operating from the grassroots upwards. To fill the vacuum, a Conference resolution in 1987 asked for (and secured in 1988) a Forum representing both front bench and Labour local authority opinion. It also included representatives from the Socialist Educational Association (SEA), which pressed for a moratorium on new voluntary schools and a commitment to a tertiary college system. But the Forum produces no policy and has functioned mainly as a sounding board for policy decisions sent from above. Among policies so sent, it turned thumbs down on magnet schooling, voluntary school extension (e.g. to new religions), and the 1991 proposals for a new 14-19 system that divided academic from vocational education. Like Conference, its power is to serve notice of continuing opinion on key issues.

c) *Policy Directorate*. It is not unusual at any one time for there to be policy differences between front bench spokespersons, the Conference, local authorities, the NEC, the Education Forum, and the Socialist Educational Association. In times past, however, the Party allowed them all an input to the education policy-making process - with the leadership retaining the right to synthesize for election manifestos. During the 1980s, however, a new policy making centre began to operate: the leader's own Policy Directorate. It gathered its own 'experts', prepared it own policy, and resolutely 'introduced' it as Labour policy. Directorate policy was generally approved - some say rubber-stamped - by Labour's National Executive (whose own policy making function was thereby curtailed). On some occasions - like *Investing in People*, 1986, and *Aiming High*, 1990 - Directorate publications did not even come to the NEC before being issued to the media. Even frontbench spokespersons were not invariably consulted. The emergence of Directorate policy - handed down from above - in place of the old process of policy emerging upwards - was a new feature of the Labour Party generally in the 1980s.

d) *Directorate Education And Training Policy*. In 1987 the Directorate published three documents bearing on education and training: *New Skills for Britain, New Jobs for Britain*, and (jointly with the TUC) *Work to Win*. They were about raising skill levels and creating new jobs in private and public sectors, but they also contained the first official education policy pronouncements for the post-14 years for some time. In particular, *New Skills* outlined Labour's plans for a 'nationally agreed core curriculum', a schools' standards council and profiles of achievement. After 16 there were proposals for a national council of courses and assessment to 'rationalize qualifications' and broaden A level. There would be a new Education and Training Inspectorate; and post-16 education would take place in tertiary networks of schools, colleges and training centres. For ages 16 and 17 there would be a 'foundation programme' that would eventually offer 'education, training and work experience to all'. After 18 there would be a programme to take increasing numbers to higher levels of qualifications in vocational education. Meanwhile, those in training schemes (entirely voluntary) would have varied length programmes, improved allowance levels, payment for work done, and there would be improved provision for women and ethic minorities. Educational maintenance allowances - related to parental income - would be available for those going on to full-time education. *New Skills* also proposed a Skillplan with a National Training Fund - which would include a 'fair contribution' from employers and joint 'workplace training teams' to audit each company's training needs and prepare plans to carry them out.

Critique

Labour's main education and training policy for the 1990s was presented in outline in these documents, although much refined since. *New Skills* registered a tentative move towards unifying education and training as well as rescuing LEAs, to whom Labour would 'restore ..responsibility for technical education in schools and all work-related FE', while also providing 'adequate resources' to help the training authority to 'undertake effective education.. ..in partnership with education services'. The proposals recognized that access to qualifications and jobs was urgent. Some of the proposals for creating jobs - like public service traineeships (e.g. housing estate officers) were particularly imaginative.

However, much of the policy seemed mere name changing - e.g. substituting Job Targeting for Job Start. Some involved no change at all - e.g. the 'tertiary networks' of colleges, schools, and training centres differed little from what already exists. Other areas signalled retreats: EMAs were now means-tested rather than universal. Paid Educational Leave for everyone was postponed indefinitely - with only a pilot programme now contemplated.

Missing from training plans was any democratic accountability. If anything, centralization was intensified, with the MSC given even more funding and control - plus new tasks it had failed previously to execute (like co-ordinating sectoral training). The ineffective Area Management Boards were left in place with their top-down appointments. There were no answers to the question of what was to happen to employees or trainees in firms with no unions. And there was a distinct lack of legislative muscle in relation to discrimination by employers and to their financial contributions to training.

Above all, planning still envisaged a divided system of academic and vocational education - still with the third layer of low-level training schemes, some of which could be retained indefinitely. Training seemed in danger of being divided into elite programmes (leading to qualifications) and those offering even less than the then-current YTS. There were no proposals in respect of private education, and none about regulating private training agencies and colleges.

Social objectives were ambiguous. Improving employers' competitiveness seemed more important than developing people and groups and meeting society's needs, and there was an unspoken acceptance of 'market forces' ideology. Proposals for control and development of training left much power in the hands of employers through a new framework of collaboration - with little acknowledgement that the interests and needs of workers and management regularly differ. Unions were given the responsibility of making training 'work in the interest of the nation', while employers had no responsibility other than to make it work in the interests of the shareholders. Even so, what were the nation's interests? Outside traditional equal opportunities and greater 'employer competitiveness', few wider social goals were elaborated - significant omissions from a Party committed to developing socialism.

However, after years of defensive inertia it was a start.

e) *Policy review and subsequent documents, 1989 - 1991.* In 1989 a single 'policy review', *Meet the Challenge, Make the Change,* covering all areas of policy, was produced by the Directorate and presented to the Labour Conference. Consultation had been a formality.

Though much-heralded as the last word, other documents (both previous and subsequent) augmented or altered the Review's commitments, including *Children First* and *Passport to Success* from 1989, *Looking to the Future, Investing in Britain's Future,* and *Aiming*

High - all from 1990 - and in addition, spokespersons continued to develop policy and the policy directorate continued to publish explanatory material (papers on the Standards Council, governing schools locally, and special needs were in preparation as we went to press).

Meet the Challenge, Make the Change restated the 1987 proposals for post-14 education and training, amalgamating these with previous 'charter' policy like home/school partnerships. While there was little new hard policy in the document (and some earlier commitments were dropped), its language was bolder and more confident, and some of its proposals - on issues like standards - were far more detailed. Its focus was also sharper, being organized around the concept of stimulating a new 'training and education culture', thus providing an up-beat answer to growing alarm from the industrial, commercial and academic establishments that Britain had fallen seriously behind the rest of the world in output of educated and trained people with a broadly based education. This same warning had been a staple part of the argument for comprehensive reform from the 1960s onwards, when many in these same groups ignored it.

f) *Policy review and after. Meet the Challenge, Make the Change* abandoned 1987's attempt to consider education and training together. It put training in the 'People at Work' section and education in 'Consumers and the Community'. The first promised a new national training strategy, the second an improvement in school standards.

Pre-five proposals, which followed the general lines of the TUC Charter (see TUC section), envisaged a reorganized system integrating (DSS) child care and (DES) education services, so that options could meet varied circumstances. It included a nursery education place for all three and four year olds, whose parents wished it. During compulsory education Labour promised a new partnership with local authorities. Fully comprehensive education would be introduced and Grant Maintained and CTC schools returned to LEA control. Assisted Places would be phased out and the 1975 Charity Commission recommendations would be enacted in relation to private schools (requiring them to meet community needs or forfeit charity status). The policy also promised to make Local Management of Schools 'effective' by giving schools more resources. All LEAs will have to have an ombudsman.

Both the National Curriculum and national testing were criticized, the first as too inflexible on foundation subjects (Labour went for a 'national core' that allowed foundation choices), the second as risking a return to a 'once-for-all pass/fail' exam. Records of Achievement would be Labour's 'centrepiece'. Another innovation would be Home/School contracts drawn up by each school. Pupils needing special education would get more teachers and more integration into the mainstream.

To raise standards, a new Education Standards Council would operate alongside a new body made up of a merger of the Schools Examination and Assessment Councils with the National Curriculum Council. The Standards Council would help develop 'yardsticks' to measure schools' performance, which LEAS would also be required to monitor, drawing up similar criteria for school 'effectiveness'. The aim would be to bring all schools up to the level of the best. There would be a new national award scheme that recognized successful schools. All schools would reflect the multi-cultural society and voluntary aided status would be granted to 'others' besides Anglicans and Catholics who qualify to run religious schools (e.g. Muslims).

Teachers would have their pay bargaining restored and a financial reward for staying on in the profession (later put at five years service or more). There would be a new core curriculum for initial teacher training and some schools would be set aside as teacher training schools. Teacher assistants would be encouraged. There would be a General Teaching Council to regulate and assist the profession.

After 16, the Standards Council would help LEAs set targets for increasing student numbers, and LEAs would have to develop plans relating to these larger numbers, and bid for funding. Students would be given two routes: either A levels (widened from three to five, as recommended by the Higginson Report of 1988) or a traineeship. The latter, which would encompass vocational education and eventually replace current youth training schemes, would be open to all ages. It would be paid for by the National Training Fund and overseen by a National Vocational Council, developing modular courses carrying credits and leading to qualifications after varying lengths of study from six months to four years - but with the first two years generally education based. A common core of English, Maths and Modern Languages would be introduced.

After 18 numbers in education and training would be extended through vocational and work-based programmes as well as in entry to higher education. A fair grants system would replace student loans. A single funding body, the 'Higher And Continuing Education Council', would be introduced to cover the 'whole post-18 education system' (*Investing*). Funding - for which institutions would bid to increase their range of entrants and run access courses - would be awarded after bidding. University lecturers would get a new system of 'tenure by merit'. The over-50s would get a programme for return to learn education on a first come, first served basis, and community education would have some 'new' initiatives funded.

Training proposals in 1989 (*Meet* and *Looking*) are an updated version of those already outlined in 1987 (*Skills* 1987). The MSC would become Skills UK and TECs would be reformed as their local 'Skill' arms. The earlier Training Teams in big companies would become Statutory Enterprise Training Councils, for which big companies would get start-up grants (small companies would have consortia) to plan training for both workers and management. Companies would be required to ensure minimum training hours. Trade Unions would have equal representation on Councils; and on local Skills agencies both LEAs and women would be appointed. There would be a new Employment Service and adult training would lose its compulsory element. Money already going to training from the government and the EEC, plus employers' contributions, would make up the New National Training Fund. There would also be a new National Advisory Body on Training. While the new traineeship was being developed, those remaining on youth training (ex-YTS) would get TU negotiated pay and all compulsion would be withdrawn. All workers would get protection under a new Workers Charter that would bring the UK into line with the collective rights enjoyed by workers in the rest of Europe. Women's needs in relation to education and training were stressed, as well as the need to devise a system catering for a variety of working life patterns - for which there will be independent training under a new Training Opportunity programme.

Today's Education and Tomorrow's Skills, 1991, enlarged considerably on previous Labour Party policy - in part to catch up with new Conservative Government moves. While still based on the policy of targets (80 per cent with GCSE A to C, and 50 per cent with A levels after) and still dividing education and training, it advocated legislation to bind employers to ensure education or training up to 18 (at least to foundation credit levels) - as well as legislation to monitor race and gender bias in education and training. There would be a single new qualification called an Advanced Certificate of Education and Training (ACET), combining 5 A levels with NVQ Level 3, organized on a modular basis with transferable credits and open to all ages. Some modules would be core ones (for education or training); others 'academic' or 'vocational' options. Consultations on how to proceed to this new system would start at once, and a possible new qualifications board that joined SEAC with NCVQ would be considered. GCSE would remain for all from 14-16 (five subjects, including technology) but the 'best' of TVEI and BTEC would also be introduced. More Compacts with employers would be introduced. The Traineeship model remains the same: qualifications based with a 'strong educational component' in the early years; and the possibility of progress to Level 4 qualifications and/or entry to higher education after four years.

Critique
Although Labour policy would provide significant improvements and go some way towards mitigating the worst features of the system which has developed under Conservatives, in many key areas there is an absence of policy. In others there is a lack of clarity about policy or conflicting commitments from policy documents and/or spokespersons' statements.

Some confusion also stems from the separation of education and training, documents having to deal twice with policy in the areas that overlap - as well as reconcile two differing ideologies. For training has industrial competition as its main objective, 'recognizing the relationship between training and profit', while education aims to meet the 'long term needs of individuals and society', recognizing the need to 'treat every child as of equal worth'. The two ideologies are not wholly compatible. Overall, a market-oriented consumerism and a 'national culture' that is narrowly restricted to 'updating' knowledge and skills, wins out over a commitment to a more equitable society, a wider individual experience, or a new international economic order.

There are areas where gaps should be filled. Pre-5 policy in the earlier documents (like *Meet*) envisaged both care and education merging and incorporating a wide variety of services, including child-minding, pre-school play groups and out of school care for older children. In later documents (like *Looking* and *Aiming*) the commitment has shrunk to one promise only, a place in nursery education for 3 and 4 year olds. Nursery places in existing schools meet the needs of some families, but by no means all, especially those who are poorer. Adding on nursery places to existing schools is not the same as reorganizing both care and education networks for the whole pre-five age group. This raises the question of whether the earlier comprehensive reorganization objectives for compulsory education (omitted from all policy after 1989) still stand.

On school issues there is a lack of clarity over key areas like the National Curriculum, testing and LMS. Earlier documents implied the first two would be substantially modified and subsequent documents would have been expected to say how. However, instead of providing more detail, they provide less. Criticism all but disappears and the impression is given that all these policies - bar a few changes like foundation-subject flexibility - would be left much as they are.

In most documents the majority of space is reserved for the issue of standards, but even here there are queries - like exactly how the Standards Council would be composed and how it would secure the improvements it would recommend. Would it use the National Curriculum's mass testing scores and exam 'results' as criteria of effectiveness? How would the planned measure of truancy rates and teacher attendance (*Aiming*) help improve standards? The danger is that these will highlight failure rather than success, or, at the very least, mischievously be misused to destroy individual schools. The same fears centre on Labour's repeated portrayal of its Teaching Council as having the central task of teacher appraisal, relating this disproportionately to dismissal. This appears to differ little from Tory teacher-testing and is hard to square with Labour's commitment to make teaching attractive enough to secure a far larger number of entrants to the profession. The same can be said of Labour policies which appear to pile an incredible load of new commitments on every teacher - including home/school contracts, a curriculum statement for each child each year, a report for each child each term, and records of achievement for all students in every year. There is no indication of what extra funding or assistance is to make any of these possible to undertake - even if the rationale for all these overlapping activities (rather than just the last, for example) were explained, which it is not.

Over Labour's plans for CTCs, opted-out schools and assisted places - commitments over which there should be no equivocation - there are several question marks, including the commitment to 'consult' the GM schools before bringing them back to LEA control. On what, for example? The same for CTCs, which in one document are 'expensive failures' (*Meet*) but in another are to be granted 'time to return.' The shadow spokesperson has even hinted they might be considered for a new special status.

Assisted places has already had to retreat, for originally Labour promised the scheme would be ended within a year. Now it is not until two parliaments have gone by. On private education the commitment has already slipped from integration (1960s) to withdrawal of charity status (1970s through Policy Review, 1989) to the latest policy which is only to review the issue. In 1989 (*Make*) private schools were seen as a 'barrier' to fully comprehensive education but in later documents (*Looking*) they are unsuitable for public money only because there are 'spare places in maintained schools,' a quite different reason. In interviews since, there have been hints that public funding may be available to private education to help them develop the National Curriculum.

Open enrolment and admissions have not been considered, nor is there any clear understanding of just what role LEAs will have in planning the development of schools and colleges and what powers and duties they will get. To restore LEAs' capacity to run a local, democratically accountable public service, requires legislation. Yet there is little commitment yet to legislation, and less to repealing significant sections of Conservatives' education acts that would be required to enact some of Labour's current commitments.

Labour has never introduced an Education Act of its own in all its 90 year history. Yet it is hard to see how Labour policy can be implemented without one. Taking one example, it would appear (*School Reorganization*, Policy Directorate Paper, November, 1990) that ending selection will be dealt with by a new circular accompanying a directive to LEAs to reorganize schools to end surplus places, rather than by legislation giving comprehensive education a positive legal status and repealing the legislation which permits schools to select by attainment. Without legislative change, it is highly likely this policy route would come to grief in the first test case brought before the courts by the hard right.

A further commitment setting out in more detail the financial resources that would be available to education also seems essential. People need to be assured that Labour's plans for the necessary improvement and expansion of the system can be accomplished. Reductions in defence expenditure are one obvious area from which funds could be switched. Even a minimal cut in public subsidies to private education would release a quite surprisingly large sum. Alternatively, there is the honest approach of saying some rise in taxation may be required - as the Liberals have done. The only other alternative is to redistribute the existing money coming to education and training in a way that funded all sections of the community more equitably. But that would require an education policy much more radical than the one Labour has chosen to date.

g) 16-19. On 16-19 education there is the same uncertainty as in earlier years about whether comprehensive reform of the system will proceed or not. In 1989 documents (like *Passport*) it is said LEAS would be 'required to produce a comprehensive post-16 education and training programme' with particular reliance on tertiary colleges. But in later ones (*Meet the Challenge*) this is reduced to LEAS only 'identifying' institutions providing a full range of education (whatever this may mean). By 1990 (*Investment*) we are even further away, for LEAS are being asked only to agree new targets about numbers staying on after 16 (in co-operation with the Standards Council). Increasing numbers and reorganizing comprehensively are two entirely different matters. At the very least, dealing with the increasingly necessary rationalization of sixth forms and tertiary institutions requires a policy commitment of some clear kind. But up to 1991 there was none (except to say tertiary colleges will be 'encouraged' (*Meet*).

Practically nothing is said either about Further Education in any of the 1989 and 1990 documents, and even if it were, the Government's new proposals for further education would require Labour's own proposals to be revised. Labour's original comprehensive commitment for 16 to 19 has so changed its nature that it is now only a commitment to 'coordinated comprehensive provision' for both full-time and part-time students and trainees in schools and colleges, the word 'comprehensive' now being used to mean the existing totality with all its divisions, rather than the 'unified, universal and comprehensive system' originally proposed (1982).

Not only is the institutional structure to remain divided after 16, so is the education inside. This is symbolized by the abandonment of the 1987 (*Skills*) commitment to a single Education and Training system with a single Inspectorate. Policy documents of 1989 claim Labour's curriculum and assessment plans for 16-19 are unifying, but they divide students down the middle between an academic route and a traineeship route. To cover this crack there is much highly confusing talk of 'equivalence', today's version of the 'parity of esteem' that was supposed to exist between grammar and secondary modern school programmes. There is no agreement about what is equivalent to what, and different policy documents carry different definitions. *Today's Education* 1991, throws it all into the melting pot once more by saying Labour will consult on all these matters as soon as it is elected.

Labour's policy of education *or* a traineeship enforces a division in the system. It is drawn from post-war Germany, with its well-known 'high road/low road' division, reflecting the perceived status of the academic and training routes. Labour's assurance that a 'mix' of vocational and academic work will be possible and that this will provide the bridge between different qualification systems, is not the same as a system built from the start as a unified one. Taking vocational qualifications into a new ACET will not solve the problem of those on a traineeship confined to a separate set of core modules. The dangers were pointed out in the Institute for Public Policy Research's *A British Baccalauréat* (1990), which argued for a single qualifications system to replace the present divided one. It tied this to a unified institutional system built around tertiary colleges (rather than Labour's retention of a school/college division). It also suggested a new Ministry of Education and Training to oversee schools, training, and higher and continuing education respectively. At 16 the only divisions would be in 'domains' like the arts or natural sciences, each one having a core, a specialized level, and a work-based level. This pattern is only one of several alternatives, but at least it is compatible with the comprehensive principle. Labour's policy has some way to go before it is even compatible.

Labour's new commitment to five subjects from 14-16 to give technological learning to all at 14-16 has meant it has had to drop humanities from the required curriculum in these vital years.

Integral to these issues is whether the new courses to be developed after 16 (and existing ones to be integrated) are to be education-led or employer-led. Here, too, Labour's policy is unclear. In earlier documents (*Skills*, 87) 'all work-related FE' will be handed back to LEAs, but more recent ones say LEAS must co-operate with employers and Skill agencies (TECs) and that the latter will 'draw up training programmes'. This bears on the issue of whether the qualifications are to be skills-based, and educationally set and assessed, or competence-based, set and assessed by employers. The difficulties in securing equivalence for the latter in any system - even under NCVQ guidance - are almost insuperable.

In 1990 a Labour frontbench spokesperson described the new traineeship as 'training with an educational element' (Gordon Brown, SEA Meeting, 1 October 1990). Why should young people (remembering the fiasco of YTS) want to stay on for this? Why should employers want to train the young people they have working for them (or in times of unemployment, employ them at all) when they can get older workers they don't have to train? These questions raise policy issues relating to education allowances, legal requirements and a selective system. Any system which depends on employers' choice will ultimately fail. The choice has to be the young person's. Payment is equally important and has undergone much change in Labour policy. Originally (1982) everyone after 16 was to get an educational maintenance allowance (with money clawed back from better-off parents). Now this has dwindled to the possibility of (means-tested) grants for those who would suffer hardship by staying on. Clearly the only way mass staying on will occur is if there is either a system of grants or well-paid waged work while education and training are taking place for those who cannot afford to stay on in education full time.

Today's Education finally ended the on/off commitment to legislate so that no school leaver can go to work without training for recognized qualifications. Such legislation is now promised. Not quite so clear is policy regarding employer contribution to training. In 1989 (*Meet*) this was firmly put as a statutory 0.5 per cent of payroll from all employers (far less than other countries require, as Labour acknowledged), but six months later (April, 1990) this was changed, apparently to get in line with CBI policy that employer contributions should be voluntary (*Skills Revolution*, 1989). The CBI claims that a skills revolution does not need more money than is already going to training schemes. But Labour is committed to raising trainees' allowances and to paying for work at TU rates. Its planned expansion of vocational education and training is ambitious. How can all this succeed without 100 per cent employer contributions at a level of at least 1 per cent?

In Labour policy documents it is clear Labour hopes to accomplish its 'revolution' in training and education by relying a lot on exhortation and subsidies. 'Labour will persuade (companies) to train.. ..by financial incentives' and Labour will rely 'on a massive change in attitude' on the part of managers and employers. But what will make them want to change when Labour's goal for them is to 'produce competitive goods and services'? Why will they wish to spend on training in future any more than they do now unless they are firmly required by law to contribute, and unless training is very firmly managed and overseen by an independent public education and training service?

As it stands, Labour is not going to put this new service in place. What we have is a return to the old centralized, top-heavy corporate structure of the MSC, with government, employers and unions operating from the top down. The local arms of the TECs have no accountability to local democratically elected bodies and they are to be filled just as AMBs used to be. In education as well there is clearly going to be excessive reliance on at least a dozen national, centralized bodies, either new or remade, rather than on local initiatives. The new national bodies include the Ombudsman network, the Educational Standards Council, the merged Curriculum Council and Assessment Council, General Teaching Council, National Vocational Council, National Advisory Body on Training, a new Employment Service, a Higher and Continuing Education Council and the Skills UK with its 100 plus arms. The introduction of these new bureaucracies augurs ill for local initiatives and institutional innovation. After 18 Labour's policy for a fair grants system has yet to explain what 'fair' actually means. Apart from the new funding Council, there is little to indicate any reform of the institutional arrangements within or between HE and FE or of the courses and pattern of study throughout higher education. The doubling of the population in these institutions is conceived largely in terms of 'adding on' to existing courses (or setting up access courses) with no acknowledgment that this huge increase will - and should - change the nature of what is learned and taught throughout higher education. There is also no acknowledgement of the need to redress the balance in course development to restore humanities and other socially important courses to an acceptable proportion of the whole in a system that has been overdriven by the market into establishing courses (many academically dubious) of short-term benefit to employers at the expense of courses of long-term benefit to individuals, the planet and human society. There is little on the restoration of research funding. On extending education to adults, the small programme for the over 50s is all that is left of the universal adult entitlement of earlier years, and reflects Labour's fears about criticism on costs. This same fear might be behind the excessively long time scale envisaged for developing vocational education traineeships for everyone: ten years. It contrasts with the short time envisaged for raising the percentage of the population with 5 GCSEs A-C from today's 30 per cent to 80 per cent: five years. Many commitments, including teachers' pay, are prefaced with the tag 'as resources permit'. Laudable as it is not to risk being tripped up by uncosted programmes, there is the equal risk of not planning with enough in hand to make many of the changes promised.

Summary of Opposition Policies

There is a consensus along quite a broad front on the need for a return to a 'partnership' between all the parties to education, to consultation of users, expansion of numbers in pre-school, post-school and adult years, to wider access, and to more resources - a large part of which should go to improving teachers' position. There is agreement about the need to end Assisted Places, CTCs and opted out schooling - as well as to restore to local authorities their capacity to plan rationally for all institutions. There is agreement on the need for a broader and more balanced curriculum entitlement - but without the rigidities of the National Curriculum. There is agreement to give adults - particularly women - more opportunities to train and study, and to insure that no young person has to leave at 16 because of poverty. There is broad agreement to upgrade vocational education all along the line, and integrate it more closely with academic education.

Almost any change in direction nationally would be an improvement, including a combination of the Liberal's education-led engine driving Labour's comprehensively-constructed machine. Even Labour's engine alone would begin to reverse a decade of damage and give rise to a great deal of hope.

Welcome as much of the alternative policy is, little of this produces any real redirection of the system. None of it is based on really radical new thinking about education and training, or the way in which society should be heading as we approach 2000. It also masks the big disagreements that remain on such matters as 'competitive' criteria for education, including testing, examinations, open enrolment; on formula funding and LMS; on religious schooling; on private schooling; and more important of all, on the deep structural inequalities relating to gender, race, class, sexuality, age and physical capacity. There is no agreement either on the various roles in education for organized parents, the churches, employers, unions, ethnic communities or, most crucially, students and pupils themselves. There is no agreement on how powers and funding should divide between the schools and colleges and the local authorities, or between the regions, including Scotland and Wales, the districts, the cities, the counties and national government. There is very little about the relationship between education in Britain and the needs of the globe or the rest of the world.

There are no detailed plans from any quarter to reorient education away from its current development as a host of competitive 'businesses', and return it to a public service, let alone direct it to different social, economic or environmental goals - or encourage it to develop the powers of individuals and groups to take control of their own lives. There is no set of proposals to infuse the system with democratic activity. There is no discussion of education and training and their relationship to international society, global needs, or the establishment of a new world economic order.

Most opposition parties have tried to promote change without directly challenging the 'captive philosophy' of Conservatism that they would inherit. So swiftly and successfully has Conservative ideology driven the system to the right that most alternative policy - and this includes Labour's - is locked on to the single goal of economic competitiveness for British employers. Even traditional liberal goals relating to individual self-development or education for its own sake, have to struggle for recognition. For this reason there is almost no change which Labour suggests - particularly in the area of standards, of which it is making so much - which Conservatives will not also try to implement themselves first.

For ten years Conservatives have been able to make continual, radical rightward change their hallmark - because they have taken care to make sure the ideas upon which their activity was based were continually argued. Unless alternative policy is based on a countervailing set of ideas - rather than on an attempt to improve or upstage Conservative policy - there is unlikely to be any serious challenge to the prevailing drift in education or society.

But equally ineffective would be calls for a halt until the 'old ways' of the 1944 partnership are dusted off and gentled back into place. A lot of Labour and liberal policy involves this response, including a reluctance to undertake any new legislation. Changes, it would appear, are supposed to come by acts of will. This is dangerous talk. Even more dangerous is the assumption that the mere absence of a Conservative government is policy enough. Even minimal change will require a popular philosophical framework. And any real Left alternative needs an identifiable ideological thrust in a new direction.

Back to Basics

We need to return to the very base of our beliefs. This means confronting the ideological base of Conservatism, particularly the claim that 'Conservatism involves the maintenance of a hierarchy and the attempt to represent the unpleasant fact of inequality as a form of natural order and legitimate.'[30] We must make manifest the meaning of Socialism as the social prospect of equality, an equally valid form of order to attempt.

We must object to the spurious notions of 'choice' and 'freedom' defined as the rights of those 'naturally' unequally-placed, to compete equally for life's chances. Survival of individuals, society and the planet requires - and always has required - democratically agreed equitable sharing. In education it involves instituting rights which everyone can enjoy - debating long and hard what these should be, and refusing to call anything a right which only the educationally knowledgeable, the socially powerful, the academically successful or the financially better-off can commandeer.

The next imperative is commitment to a public education and training service - as a social good. Making the case for a public service means making the case against leaving matters to 'the market'. Evidence against the market's capacity to manage the system is strewn across the face of education and training. It must be marshalled in the cause of argument for specific types of planning, an activity that has all but disappeared from education and training, overwhelmed as it is now by directives. These require neighbour to fight neighbour as the only means of settling the distribution of resources. Planning should be in the interests of the whole community rather than based on superior pressure by the most favoured - and it should be without any return to the bureaucratic benevolence of the 1944 Act.

Thus a third imperative is making the case for democratic accountability - from the bottom up - ending our institutional inertia. There must be new forms of educational delivery, organized in new ways locally and nationally. It means professionals and users - with only minimal messages from the Centre - taking a much greater responsibility for devising, executing and assessing education and training - and working together to plan their own learning. It is wrong that the power to set out what may or may not be taught - and to assess its effectiveness - should reside wholly outside the classroom and be denied to those who teach and learn inside it. It means taking action continually to monitor the system ourselves - against our own agreed outcomes - taking our own action when there is failure or success rather than waiting passively for others to set up bureaucracies to tell us what we already know but are prevented from dealing with because we are denied both democratic means and economic resources.

The third imperative is for a goal of equality explicitly explained as not making everyone alike but exactly the reverse: recognizing the barriers that prevent individuals, groups, nations and societies from having their own fair and equal share - having their rights - and taking action to remove the barriers. It is common sense not to allow people to believe that they are powerless in the face of change, since the point of all education and training should be to give people the power to change - personally and collectively - in ways that make common sense.

We need to face intolerance much more squarely in education, citing its relationship to a philosophy of inequality which forces communities, individuals and groups to forego what should belong to them as of right; and a pedagogy which ensures the dismissal of so many so early from the chance of educational success and enjoyment and preparation for work they really want to learn to do. Conservativism requires failure to feed its development and protect the privileged. That is its fatal flaw. A socialist education system's great advantage should be that it cannot afford to allow anyone to fail.

On these principles we can build and translate our ideas into concrete educational practice.

Notes

1. Angela Rumbold suggested a 'half GCSE' for lower levels of attainment in 1989.
2. Rhodes Boyson, among many, has advocated this for some years. See *The Times Educational Supplement*, 6 October 1989.
3. See the Centre for Policy Studies (CPS) report quoted in *The Times Educational Supplement*, 6 October 1989.
4. *Education in the 1990s*, a Carlton Paper 1991.
5. As incoming Tories did when they took control of Ealing in 1990.
6. As was done, albeit indirectly, at Brighton Polytechnic in 1989
7. Suggested by Rhodes Boyson in *The Daily Mail*, 3 June 1989. He called it 'Thatcherism at Work'.
8. Claus Moser, 1990; *Towards a Skills Revolution*, 1989.
9. See the report in *The Guardian*, 31 March 1987.
10. *Education in the 1990s*, a Carlton Paper, 1991.
11. See Anthony O'Hear's chapter in *The GCSE: An Examination*, (edited by Joanne North), the Claridge Press, 1987 and Mervyn Hiskett, *Choice in Rotten*

Apples: Bias in GCSE Examining Groups, Centre for Policy Studies, 1988.

12. See Anthony O'Hear 'Black Marks for GCSE' in *The Times Educational Supplement,* 6 October 1989.

13. See the Goldsmiths' Media Department Research.

14. See, for example, the Report of the Curriculum Complaints Panel, 22 November 1990, Ealing. This rejects a case brought by the Campaign for Real Education against multi-faith education in a local school.

15. *The Yorkshire Post,* 29 June 1989.

16. See, for example, *Education and Indoctrination,* edited by Roger Scruton, Angela Ellis Jones and Dennis O'Keefe, Education Research Centre, 1985.

17. See, for example Sheila Lawlor's article in *The Daily Telegraph,* 18 November 1989.

18. See Stuart Deucher's *History and GCSE History,* Centre for Policy Studies, 1987.

19. Mervyn Hiskett, *Choice in Rotten Apples: Bias in GCSE Examining Groups,* Centre for Policy Studies, 1988.

20. NUT, *A Strategy for the Curriculum,* 1990.

21. AUT, *Widening Opportunities,* 1982.

22. See, for example, *Goodwill Under Stress,* 1990.

23. *Childcare and Nursery Education,* a TUC Charter, 1989.

24. *Putting Pupils First,* No 3 Federal Paper; *Higher Education, Investing in Our Future,* No 14, 1990; *The Learning Society,* No. 5, 1990.

25. *Green Party Policy- Education* and *Green Party Education Working Group: Education,* both undated but sent to enquirers in 1990; and *Manifesto for a Sustainable Society,* 1990.

26. *Policy Summary No 1* and *SNP Priorities for Scottish Education,* both 1990.

27. *Wales in Europe* and *Programme for the 90s,* both sent 1990.

28   *The National Labour Movement Inquiry into Education, Training and Unemployment,* Birmingham Trade Union Resources Centre, 1987.

29. *Socialist Standard,* October, 1989, published by the Socialist Party of Great Britain.

30. Roger Scruton, *The Meaning of Conservatism,* 1980.

Chapter Three

The Structure of the System: Proposals for Change

Andy Green

Introduction

An effective and egalitarian education system is one designed to promote the highest levels of achievement and individual development in all children and adults, regardless of class, ethnicity, religion, gender, sexual orientation or disability. Such a system must, by definition, give all children and students access to the same learning experiences. This does not mean that all must be subject to an identical or uniform experience: individuals will differ in some of their educational needs and priorities, depending on their personalities, the communities or regions from which they come, and the career choices they make as they approach adulthood. However, in a democratic society, everyone must have a right or entitlement to certain fundamental benefits that education can confer and which a participatory democracy needs in its citizens, if it is to function as such. Socialists have long argued, in this and other countries, that such universal ends can be achieved only through a comprehensive - that is all-embracing - system and that the comprehensive principle must extend to *both* the institutional structure *and* the curricula that it is designed to deliver.

Both of these are equally significant if the aims of comprehensive education are to be achieved. The advocates of comprehensive education in Britain in the 1960s rightly stressed the importance of developing all-inclusive institutions but often paid less attention to the development of curricula which would be appropriate to this new comprehensive intake of students. Such an approach would have been anathema to Socialist policy-makers in continental states, like France and Sweden, where a common national curriculum has always been seen as an essential pre-requisite for comprehensive schooling, and it greatly undermined the effectiveness of the comprehensive movement in this country. This lesson would now appear to have been learnt and in recent years attention has shifted more towards the design of a curriculum suitable for comprehensive institutions and capable of offering equal opportunities to all students. Despite the continuing disagreements about the relative merits of a 'national', 'common', or common core curriculum, this is an important step forward. However, it is no less important to continue to press for further institutional reorganization of our system since it is still far from comprehensive in its design and falls far short of providing equal opportunities for all.

Despite the spread of comprehensive schools in the 1970s, the education system in Britain is still multiply fragmented and in some areas remains so incoherent that it barely deserves the title of a system at all. Scotland has traditionally shared more of the universalist, rationalist spirit of continental education and, with pervasive comprehensive organization, fewer independent schools, and less regional differentiation, has a more uniform structure; however, the institutional diversity of education in England and Wales is renowned and quite unique. Amongst its more obvious peculiarities are the exceptional level of autonomy afforded to independent schools, universities and private examining bodies; the sharp divisions between the private and public sectors, and the no less significant duality of church and county schools in the maintained sector; and the enormous gulf that separates the provision of education and training in both sectors. Despite the shift towards comprehensive institutions, the maintained sector is far from uniform since local authorities have adopted different organizational models - some with all-through secondary schools, some with middle school systems, and yet others with community schools - and the diversity has now been extended with the creation of Grant Maintained Schools and City Technology Colleges. In the system of post-16 education and training the plurality of institutions is little short of chaotic. Upper secondary education has never been comprehensive. Over 15 per cent of those participating have always been in the private sector (over 40 per cent in some LEAs), and until recently less than a third of state school pupils stayed on. Those who do stay on go to a wide variety of different institutions including sixth forms, traditional and 'new', sixth form consortia, sixth form colleges, tertiary colleges, further education colleges, and a host of different training schemes run by various agencies both public and private.

The institutional diversity and fragmented nature of education in England has a very long history. The Bryce Commission noted in 1895 that 'freedom, variety and elasticity' were the hallmarks of English education, adding, quite correctly, that its 'growth ha(d) not been either continuous or coherent' and that there was a great need for a system with a 'coherence.. ..an organic relation between different authorities and different kinds of school.'[1] England was exceptionally late to develop a central authority for education in the 19th century and did not achieve anything like an integrated national education system until 1902, almost a century after France and the German states. Amongst the main reasons for this had been liberal hostility towards state involvement in education, and a determination of powerful interest groups, like the churches and the 'public' schools, to maintain their autonomy. When a national system did finally emerge it was more an aggregation of different parts than a rationally planned whole, and a high level of autonomy was preserved for the universities, public schools, church schools and for other private bodies like the City and Guilds and the examination boards.

Another hallmark of the liberal tradition has been the preference of governments for 'permissive' legislation, that is to say legislation which empowers the responsible authorities to make reforms without directing them to do so, or, in many cases, without giving them the wherewithal to do so. Given the conservatism and ineptitude which many governments have displayed when planning for education, this form of legislation has naturally seemed a boon to local authorities and indeed to most progressives in education. However, it has also contributed considerably to the fragmented and unco-ordinated development of the system, and has often meant that when legislation has been of a progressive nature it has not been speedily or fully implemented. There are numerous historical examples of this. The 1870 Forster Education Act provided for the setting up of local school boards and the board schools but left the important matter of compulsory attendance to local discretion; the 1889 Technical Instruction Act allowed the new local authorities to levy a rate for technical schooling but did not oblige them to do so which meant that it was a long time before most made use of the provision; and the 1902 Balfour Education Act permitted but did not instruct local authorities to create county grammar schools - again delaying the implementation of reform.

Post-war educational history has been dominated by the settlement reached with the 1944 Education Act which brought in, amongst other things, universal secondary education. Although in some ways a watershed, this Act was also very much in line with the old liberal traditions in education. It created a structure of educational administration officially designated as 'a national system, locally administered' and popularly understood as 'decentralized'. This characterization often obscures as much as it illuminates - conveniently ignoring for instance the limits placed on local autonomy by underfunding and the stranglehold of the universities and examination boards. However, it does point to one enduring peculiarity of the system which has been its obdurately fragmented nature. Whatever the benefits of relative local autonomy, and these are particularly cherished now that they are close to extinction, a heavy price has been paid in incoherence. Government planning for co-ordination of the system has continued to be weak in various areas and permissive legislation has continued to be a two-edged sword.

By not giving serious consideration to the structure or curriculum of the new secondary schools the Butler Act paved the way for the problems which followed when it was implemented according to a tripartite plan as recommended by the 1943 Norwood Report. The result was the three-tier system of secondary schools which was not only highly divisive and unfair in its rigid adherence to selection at the 11 plus, but which also failed to work even on its own terms. The new modern and technical secondary schools lacked the clear purpose and distinctive ethos which, for instance, made the Realschule and Hauptschule in Germany's similarly hierarchical system, though still divisive, relatively successful and enduring. The technical schools thus never really took off and the resultant *de facto* binary system caused so much anguish amongst the majority of parents, whose children were consigned to the modern schools, that the pressure grew, not least amongst middle-class parents, for a comprehensive system. This then developed through the initiative of progressive local authorities. However, when the comprehensive movement received central government sanction in 1965 the failure to prescribe a unified organizational model or any kind of common curriculum robbed the system of much of the coherence and purpose necessary to make it work. Whilst comprehensive lower secondary education spread to most local authorities in time, the upper secondary system was never remotely comprehensive. Lack of central government planning was again a critical failing. In the early 1970s the DES did little to plan the development of post-16 education, as its counterparts on the continent were doing. An OECD investigation of the DES which published its findings in 1975 expressed consternation at this complacency and described provision for 16-19s as so 'typically British in its flexibility and empiricism,' that it was 'hard to describe as a system.'[2] With the growth of youth unemployment in the late 1970s it was clear that something had to be done about post-16 provision, but in the absence of any clear plan, reform was limited to a series of *ad hoc* panic measures, each of which failed only to be replaced by some equally temporary measure.

The Conservative Government seems determined to achieve the worst of both worlds. Its authoritarian and centralist approach, embodied in the 1988 Education Act, has forfeited many of the strengths of the old 'decentralized system' - endangering local initiative and creativity by demoralizing the teachers and disempowering the local authorities, and sabotaging the one potentially good measure which might have come out of such legislation, the adoption of a common curriculum, through the failure to consult and achieve a consensus over the content of that curriculum. On the other hand, the long-term agenda of the Government is clearly to create a 'free-market' education system, the centralization of control being merely a vehicle for removing the state as far as possible from education and creating a largely private system. Essentially this is a 19th century liberal programme which would take us back to all the problems of fragmentation, incoherence, and complacency which beset *laissez-faire* education policies then, and whose legacy we have never quite superseded.

The problem with a *laissez-faire* or free-market approach to a service like education is not just that it results in unsystematic and rather untidy networks of provision, a kind of British muddle rather unseemly to the rational technocratic eye. It is that it is unjust, ineffective and often inefficient. Free market gurus, like Stuart Sexton, criticise contemporary schooling for its bureaucracy, state monopoly and lack of competition.

'The present parlous state of state maintained education,' he wrote in 1987, 'is not the result of six years of Conservative Government, it is the result of thirty years or more of successive government attempts to run education as a government managed service.'[3] The truth, in fact, is quite the opposite. The system has never been sufficiently managed by the elected public authorities, and has also been too much dominated by powerful private interest groups. The problems did not so much originate in post-war social democracy but in the liberal policies of the previous hundred years. It is now manifestly clear that continental education systems, like those of France, Germany and Sweden, achieve considerably higher all-round standards in education and training with the majority of their students, than is the case in Britain. It is no accident that each of these systems has a far higher degree of 'state management' and planning than has been the case in Britain. It would be hard to find an example of a successful 'free-market' education system. Richard Lynn has recently tried to argue the case for Japan but most unconvincingly. That system does indeed achieve high standards with most pupils, especially in mathematical and scientific areas, but it is hardly a paragon of free-enterprise schooling. While upper secondary education is indeed partly independent and fee-paying, up to the age of 15 all children go to schools which are free, comprehensive and totally unstreamed, and which are subject to a national curriculum.[4]

Outside of the English-speaking world, where free-market ideas have made most headway, there is in fact little evidence of the countries actually moving towards free market education systems. In continental Europe there is no obvious equivalent to local school management (LMS) or competition between educational institutions, at least during the compulsory stage of education, and educational planning, involving different 'social partners', is still considered axiomatic. Education and training are seen as a public service to which it is inappropriate to apply the mechanisms of the market. There are a number of reasons why this is so.

A market education system would be both inefficient and, in national terms, ineffective. The inefficiency results from multiple overlaps in provision and waste of resources where services are not planned. Education is a relatively inelastic process involving heavy investment in fixed capital (buildings and equipment) and in human capital (trained teachers) and these investments cannot be transferred speedily to respond to changing local demand resulting from demographic change and shifting patterns of consumer choice. A good example of this inefficiency in our emerging educational market lies in the overlaps in provision in the post-16 sector and in the large number of surplus school places which LEAs are unable to remove due to the way in which 'opting-out' and open-enrolment have undermined their planning powers. Whilst effective in parts (the privileged parts), market education systems are likely to be ineffective in meeting society's overall needs (for high levels of education and training amongst all citizens) because they do not recognize overarching collective needs, concentrating, as they do, only on individual choices. Demand-led systems also tend to be backward looking or at least myopic and therefore rarely set strategic goals for future development. This is because consumer demand is often based on short term considerations, as is often the case with employers, or based on aspirations which have been forged historically, as with parents and their own educational experiences.

Free-market systems are also fundamentally undemocratic. This may seem paradoxical since they are based on choice. However, free choice in education is not like choice in the purchase of other commodities. First, education is an inherently collaborative enterprise, and cannot be reduced to individualized choices. Children learn in classes, and their learning depends on other students. Second, the exercise of choice by some parents, better positioned than others to make certain choices, limits the choices available to others. For instance, if middle class parents decide to take their children out of a local school, this may effect the quality of education in that school and limit the chances of a good education for those that remain. Third, the choices being made in education are largely those of the parents not the children, who are the real consumers. This is the democracy of parent power, where parental choice is premised on ownership of children. A more genuine and future-oriented democracy would be based on a concept of children as citizens-in-the-making. Children should have basic rights such that their education and futures are not limited as a result of choices made by parents based on circumstances and culturally determined aspirations.

Lastly, market education systems are inherently unequal and hierarchical. This is for the simple reason that choice depends on the purchasing power, aspiration and market knowledge of the consumers, the parents, and these are not evenly spread around. Market mechanisms in education would lead to a multiply-tiered range of schools where some would provide élite education for those who could afford it or knew how to select it, and others would enter into a spiral of decline and provide very poor education. A fragmented mixed system, like our own, cannot avoid reproducing inequality in a stratified society. Class, race and gender inequalities invariably appear through the cracks in the system. The strength of the more universalist, comprehensive system is that it places more equal normative expectations on all children thus attempting to counteract other social forces which will tend to stream and segregate children into different tracks with different expectations thus reproducing social inequalities.

The main sources of institutional division in our current system lie with the 'public' and other semi-independent schools, with the voluntary schools, and with the separation between education and training. The public schools are the most singular and elitist of British institutions, seen by overseas observers as the symbol of everything that is most anachronistic and peculiar about British society and even by the British public as 'another country' in their own land. Other countries have private schools: indeed in France and the USA, the pioneer of democratic education, at least 15 per cent are educated privately compared with over 7 per cent in Britain. What is distinctive about the British public schools is not that they offer a particular kind of education to a socially privileged minority, but that they carry such overwhelming prestige and influence. French and American private schools exist for religious minorities, and sometimes for their social status, but they do not confer the enormous privileges on their beneficiaries guaranteed by the British public schools.

French Catholic Schools were long ago cut down to size by Napoleon who wanted the state to control the best schools to ensure the middle class their careers open to talent. Catholic secondary schools were limited to only one in each department where there was no lycée and were compelled to pay a tax to the Université, the administrative engine of the state system. Meanwhile the state lycées were developed to the point where they outclassed the catholic schools in academic prestige and popularity. Even King Louis Philippe sent his own children to the lycée. Such a situation would have been inconceivable in Britain where, on the contrary, everything has been done to ensure the pre-eminence and independence of the public schools. They have remained almost entirely free from state control even to this day and in fact receive enormous concealed subsidies from the state. This is not only a matter of their tax exemption deriving from so-called 'charitable status', but also of the subsidies gained from government assisted places, the employment of teachers trained at the expense of the state, and the grants paid to numerous categories of senior military and diplomatic personnel so that their children can receive private education. A recent estimate puts the amount of public money going into the independent school sector at £1.3 bn per annum.[5]

The public schools give enormous privileges to the children of the well-off. A mere 7 per cent of the nation's children still monopolize nearly half the places at Oxford and Cambridge universities and a large share of the top positions in the state and government. However, the problem is not simply that they perpetrate undemocratic and reactionary values in the ruling élites and allow a minority of parents to buy life chances for their children; they also damage the state sector. So long as a large section of the ruling class in our society has no investment in state schools, the future of public sector education will be insecure. As R. H. Tawney once remarked, English education policy has for the most part been determined 'by men few, if any, of whom have themselves attended the schools principally effected by it, or would dream of allowing their children to attend them.'[6] This is still true of Conservative governments today. Although not all of the present Cabinet themselves went to an independent school, few of them entrust their children to the state schools which they manage.

Whilst the public schools have thrived in recent years from increased government support and growing enrolments, further ballast has been added to the independent sector through the establishment of a new tier of semi-independent schools. The new Grant Maintained Schools and City Technology Colleges are still officially within the maintained sector and are not, as yet, fee-charging, but they enjoy exceptional privileges and autonomy and the CTCs are not even subject to the National Curriculum. The average capital allocation, for instance, for Grant

Maintained Schools in 1989 was £276,000 as against £15,000 on average for 25,000 other maintained schools in the country.[7] The estimated accumulated cost to the exchequer by 1993 for the projected 20 City Technology Colleges will be a massive £170m.[8] Such lavish resourcing will ensure that a small minority of children enjoy exceptional facilities whilst the majority of schools are reduced to petitioning their parents for donations to provide essential books and computer hardware.

Another historic division within the maintained sector in this country is that between voluntary schools and county schools. The voluntary schools are the most visible inheritance from the 19th *laissez-faire* tradition. They owe their survival into the 20th century to a deal struck with Balfour's Conservative Government, by which they conceded some local authority control in return for rate aid, and to a House of Lords veto on a 1906 Liberal bill to secularize state education. Today a third of maintained schools are still voluntary. In general they have greater autonomy than do county schools, although their level of independence varies according to whether their legal status is 'aided', 'controlled' or 'special agreement'. In aided schools, for instance, governors have the right to appoint and dismiss staff according to religious criteria, whereas in controlled schools they have such rights only in relation to teachers of RE. The voluntary schools certainly do not constitute such a divisive force as do the private schools and the majority accede to the policies of the local authorities which fund them. However, in some cases they have been shown to undermine egalitarian policies. Voluntary secondary schools were generally somewhat slower to go comprehensive, particularly the non-denominational ones which constitute almost a third of the total, and voluntary aided schools still have the right to reject LEA plans for them and can, therefore, make LEA planning difficult. There is also evidence that in some cases voluntary schools have used the privilege they have to admit on the basis of religion to gain more than the average of Band 'A' pupils or to take less than the average proportion of non-white pupils for their area.[9]

Another, more damaging, division in British education is that between education and training after 16. This also goes back to the 19th century when academic secondary education was reserved for the middle and upper classes, while the rest made do with primary education followed, in some cases, by an apprenticeship or evening classes run by the Department of Science and Art or the Mechanics

Institutes. The same division existed in all European countries but in Britain became particularly entrenched. This was partly because of the split between the anti-utilitarian classical values of the gentry-run public and grammar schools and the narrowly empirical ethos and low status accorded to technical education; it was also exacerbated again by the *laissez-faire* ideology which encouraged the delegation of all responsibility for training to the employers thus exempting the government from any serious involvement to the end of the century. No continental tradition of state-run trade schools evolved, which meant that training became normatively part-time, work-based and low status, sharply divided from mainstream education.

This division still exists today, despite a century of technical college education. Typically, after finishing compulsory schooling the middle-class child continues in education, whilst the working-class child goes into some kind of training. In the last two decades post-compulsory education and training has developed something like a tripartite structure. Sixth forms and sixth-form colleges mainly offer a general education dominated by A levels and the old grammar school tradition, preparing young people for professional and managerial roles. They still represent an élite track where less than a quarter of young people stay the course. At the other extreme there are the youth training schemes and college- or school-based pre-vocational courses for the majority of school leavers which offer a limited general education combined with training, the latter very narrow and job-specific in the case of Youth Training. Sandwiched in the middle is a thin layer of BTEC courses which offer a combination of general and vocational education, aimed at technician and junior managerial levels in most cases.

This separation of post-16 education and training is enormously impoverishing for all concerned. As the Higginson and BP Reports have recently suggested, the A level route is too elitist, too narrow, too specialized and is in no-one's best interests, except perhaps that it maintains a privileged highway to higher education for the middle class. The vocational sector provides a preparation which is too limited and too job specific for what is required in many areas of the modern economy. The division between the two perpetuates social inequalities and limits choice, and this, together with the sheer unintelligibility of the system for most young people, must bear a large share of responsibility for the fact that Britain has amongst the lowest participation rates in 16-19 education and training in Europe.

The split that has existed between polytechnics and universities in higher education derives from the same historic division between liberal and technical education. When the Labour Government set about expanding higher education in the 1960s it ignored the recommendations of the 1963 Robbins Report for a unified system, and opted instead for the binary model. Universities would continue to concentrate on the liberal arts and pure science whilst the new polytechnics would be devoted to applied science and vocational subjects. Whatever the justification for this decision then things did not turn out that way and polytechnic teaching and research now cover exactly the same range of subjects as in the universities. The only real material difference is that students and staff in polytechnics have to make do with fewer resources than do those in the universities. Here as elsewhere in the education system diversity is merely a mask for status distinctions and social privilege.

Proposals for Action

In the light of these existing problems there is now a case for a thoroughgoing reorganization of the institutional structure of our system, along with reforms in curricula and examinations. Our recommendations can be categorized according to the different stages of education.

Pre-school

Lack of pre-school and child-care provision is one of the major obstacles to equal opportunities between men and women, restricting women's opportunities to study, seek and retain paid employment, participate in public life, recreation and leisure.[10] Children are also denied equal chances to prepare educationally and socially for school and to receive supervised care after school. As demographic changes reduce the supply of young people for work, inadequate pre-school and child care provision also reduces the possibilities for employers to make good the skills shortages by increasing the employment of parents with responsibility for young children.

Pre-school provision in Britain is not good by European standards. It is true that some 81 per cent of three and four year olds receive some kind of full or part-time education or day-care, an overall participation rate only exceeded by Belgium and France. However, 40 per cent of these were not receiving education and a further 21 per cent are those admitted to primary school early. The proportion of those receiving a genuinely pre-school education is thus barely 20 per cent, well below Italy, and a long way behind the 83 per cent in France and Belgium.[11] What is more, access to this is very unevenly distributed. A child in a Labour area, for instance, has twice the chance of a nursery place as a child in a Conservative or Liberal Democrat area. The fragmentation and lack of co-ordination of provision also mean that many parents are not aware of the different options and what they actually represent.

The way forward in this area must involve both expansion and greater integration of provision. There should be a statutory duty on all local authorities to provide a comprehensive, flexible and integrated child care/education provision for the under fives and out of school care for 5-14 year olds. With the removal of tax on work-place nurseries, there will also be opportunities for partnerships between local government employers and voluntary agencies to develop suitable provision where appropriate.

Primary and Secondary

A number of reforms in primary and secondary school organization are necessary if we are to move towards a genuinely comprehensive provision. These relate to the boundaries between primary, secondary and tertiary education; the role and status of voluntary schools; the regulation of private education; the transfer of CTCs and Grant Maintained Schools back to local authority control; and the integration of special education into the mainstream.

The existing boundaries between different levels or stages of education are variable and confusing and are often drawn in a way that is detrimental to the educational progress of the child. These boundaries need to be reconsidered and harmonized throughout the system.

Many would argue that the institutional break between primary and secondary education at 11 is not in the best interests of most children. The transfer is often a traumatic experience and consequently the progress of many children suffers in the early years of secondary school. There is a strong argument therefore for softening the transition through the integration of primary and secondary schools into unitary networks. This would involve greater administrative and curricula harmonization, although not necessarily geographical concentration. To create single all-purpose campuses for these stages in every locality would be prohibitively expensive and would also involve in many cases an unwelcome centralization of primary school sites, increasing travelling distances for young children. A preferable solution would be for a single school network involving secondary level 'departments', with smaller satellite primary departments, as is sometimes done with the Swedish all-through 7-16 Grundskolan.

The upper boundary of secondary education also needs to be reconsidered. At present arrangements vary *within* and *between* different authorities. Some children continue in the secondary school sixth-form or sixth-form consortium until 17 or 18; others leave at 16 for work or to go to college or onto a training scheme. Such a diversity of practices is not only confusing; it also undermines the development of any normative expectations for children at this age, encouraging too many to be tempted by the prospect of an early wage into leaving education and training altogether at 16. This diversity of routes also impedes the integration of education and training at the tertiary level.

There is a very strong case for instituting a nationwide break at 16 years, as is the practice in many other countries. The age marks both the end of school-based GCSE study for most young people and the end of compulsory education and is therefore a significant moment for them both socially and educationally. It is also a significant age for young people in terms of their personal development and one at which many would prefer to make a transition to an institution with a more adult environment. This is not, of course, always the case and some young people would prefer to continue their sixth-form studies in an institution with which they are already familiar and in which they have come to play a important and more responsible role. Clearly no one transition point will suit everyone equally. However, there are other over-riding reasons for instituting a break at this age which concern the coherence and quality of what is offered at the tertiary or post-16 level. If the objective is to achieve a comprehensive tertiary provision for 16-19s, which integrates education and training, (for which the case is argued below), then there has to be a general transition at 16 since most schools are not able to offer the range of subjects, especially in vocational education, which would make this a reality.

The time is clearly opportune for instituting such a break as the national practice. Falling roles have already reduced the size of most sixth-forms to a point where they are either uneconomic or educationally restrictive. The range of subjects that can be offered by most school sixth-forms now is quite unacceptably narrow, unless class sizes are very small. In that case the cost of the generous teacher-pupil ratios has to be matched by savings lower down the school. Separating secondary and tertiary education by a break at 16 would appear to be the best solution educationally and the most efficient. Any wholesale change to this practice would clearly have to be phased in over a period of time. It would also have to be managed in a way that took account of the understandable sensitivities of school teachers for whom the work of the sixth-form is often highly prized. We make recommendations on these points below.

The question of the status of the voluntary schools also needs urgent attention. In a society which is becoming increasingly secular and, at the same time, increasingly multi-faith, the justification for granting a special status to every third school because of its religious affiliations seems more historical than just or logical. Not only are the privileges granted to voluntary schools sometimes used in ways which undermine equal opportunities, but they also represent a provocative anomaly to religious groups who have not been accorded the privileges given historically to groups like the Anglican and Catholic Churches. The solution to this, in our view, is neither to abolish them completely nor to extend their privileges to all other religious groups which might wish to set up their own schools with similar rights to state support. The first course would involve unrealistic costs, involving the state in buying the land and buildings of some 8000 schools from their current owners. The second course would involve multiplying the divisive effects of the present system for the sake of consistency in applying a principle of denominational schooling which we do not, in any case, wholeheartedly support.

The alternative solution is to allow voluntary schools to remain in the hands of their existing owners but to make state financial support conditional on those schools accepting the same regulations and policies which are applied in the county schools. The rights of voluntary schools to select their pupils and staff according to religious criteria should therefore cease. All children, of whichever religion, or no religion, should have equal rights to go any school of their choice, subject to places being available and the local authority's need to balance the ability intake of their schools. Preference should be given to children who wish to utilize their right to a place at their named local school (see Proposals for a New Education Act). All schools, including the voluntary schools, should be committed to equal opportunities and be party to the same multi-cultural, multi-faith policies. There is already evidence of some support for such a policy in both the Anglican and Catholic Churches and in time more may come to see it as preferable to outright abolition or total independence. Such a policy would need legislation and the instigation of a Harmonization Commission to plan for and oversee the transition for the voluntary schools.[12]

As with the voluntary schools, but to a far greater degree, the independent private schools also undermine the development of equal opportunities in education. This has been acknowledged by several commissions and Labour Governments in the past, but no effective action has ever been taken. This may have been due to lack of political will on the part of governments, to the absence of agreement on strategy, or to the gulf between rhetoric and reality which has often characterized the debate. In any case the priority now must be to look for a viable solution which might conceivably be adopted and implemented.

Two proposals which have been canvassed frequently in the past seem to us to have little credibility. Outright abolition would seem to be impossible. In a democratic society individuals cannot be denied the right to pay for educational tuition from independent providers if they so wish. Any such proscription would eliminate not only the public schools but also the WEA, private language schools and private tuition in numerous subjects not always provided in the maintained sector, like homeopathy, acupuncture, adult fitness, music and so on. On the other hand, proposals to reduce the divisiveness of the public schools by trying to 'integrate' them in various ways with the state system seem unlikely to work. Spending public funds on assisted places for a few children, usually from middle class families, does nothing to democratize public schools. On the contrary, it strengthens their privileged position by increasing their intake, by giving them spurious meritocratic legitimacy, and by weakening the state sector through creaming off able pupils. Making the charitable status of public schools conditional on their providing services to the state sector, like the use of laboratories and sports facilities, would equally strengthen their position. It would give credence to the morally baseless claim that they are in fact charities in the normal meaning of the term, whilst granting little advantage to the state schools, few of whose pupils would relish the position of being temporary guests picking the crumbs from the high table of élite education. Better that the public school pupils should be guests in the classrooms of state schools.

It has been said that in the end the only answer to the problem of élitist private schools is to make the state schools better. There is much to be said for this view since the problem is not so much about the existence of this minority of institutions, whatever one may think of them, but rather about the disproportionality of their influence and the inequality between them and the state schools. Improving the quality and prestige of state schools would clearly diminish both of these phenomena. The measures proposed in this volume for the reform of state education are, of course, designed to do just that.

However, this does not mean that the situation with regard to the independent schools should remain just as it is. Private schools should cease to receive any overt or covert subsidies from the state, as befits institutions upholding the free-market ethic. This would mean the withdrawal of charity status tax exemption, the abolition of assisted places, and an end to the practice whereby the state pays for the private school fees of military and diplomatic children. Private schools should also pay a levy towards the cost of all aspects of the public education service from which they benefit, like Her Majesty's Inspectorate, DES research and statistics, teacher training and so on. The private preparatory and secondary schools should also be subject to the terms of any common core or national curriculum applicable to the maintained sector. The same should apply to private school sixth-forms in the case of any statutory common core curriculum developed for 16-19 education and training. Legislation would be required to put this into effect.

The City Technology Colleges and Grant Maintained Schools, like the private schools, undermine equal opportunities and absorb high levels of public funding which could be put to better use in improving the resourcing of local authority comprehensive schools. They should be reabsorbed into the local authority system and the legislation on which they are based should be reversed.

With regard to children with special educational needs, the principles of integration enshrined in the 1981 Act should now be put into effect. This means that extra resources and facilities should be provided for schools to make them appropriate environments for children with special needs. It will remain for the parents and local authorities to decide jointly, on the basis of the individual child, and the special needs involved, where he or she should be educated. In some cases this will continue to mean separate schooling in special schools, because this is the best possible environment for that child. However, in so far as adequate funding can provide the right facilities and expertise in mainstream schools, children with special needs will be educated alongside other children in comprehensive schools.

Tertiary

Post-compulsory education and training is the area in most need of thoroughgoing structural reform. We have already indicated some of the problems in the present mixed system. The academic A level 'route' through the sixth-forms and sixth-form colleges is an élitist hang-over from an era which did not truly believe in mass education, at least not beyond the elementary level. It is unsuitable for the majority of pupils, involves too much early and unbalanced specialization, and reinforces a distinction between general theoretical education and applied vocational education which is in no-one's interests. On the other hand, most of what currently passes for vocational education or training is too narrowly practical and too job-specific. The division between the two is not only socially divisive; it also represents a form of preparation for adult life which is out of tune with modern social and economic realities. Modern economies increasingly require employees with a good broad general education and skills which are transferable between processes, plants and technologies. Our system produces the opposite. It has been described in a recent report from the Institute for Public Policy Research as an 'early-selection, low-participation system', the concomitant of low-skill, low productivity economy.[13]

To achieve an economy based on what economists call 'high value-added, high-technology production,' means creating a high-participation, late-specialization system of education and training after compulsory education.

A number of alternatives have been proffered for the post-16 sector. Some involve more free-market business control in training, as with the government's new Training and Enterprise Councils, and are unlikely to work for the same reasons *laissez-faire* policies have never worked in training. Some, like the Higginson proposals for a broadened A level, move in the right direction but too cautiously, and offer no solution to the fundamental problem of the division between education and training. Other, more far reaching proposals, like Labour's plan for a German-style training system, are equally misplaced. That 'Dual System' of training, although considerably better and more widespread than previous apprenticeship systems have been in Britain, has considerable problems and would be unlikely to work here even on its own terms. It is a hierarchical and inflexible system which concentrates too heavily on job-specific skills and transferred to Britain it would fail, not least because of the lack of employer commitment and trained instructors here.

The best strategy in Britain for increasing levels of education and training in the post-16 sector would be to create an integrated, education-led system, combining education and training in a single framework of institutions, curricula and assessment. At the institutional level this would require the end of sixth-forms and sixth-form colleges, which are unable to offer most technical subjects, and the abolition of youth training schemes, which offer little general education and only narrow skills training. The current mixture of institutions should be replaced by a comprehensive system of colleges able to offer the full range of academic and technical subjects on a full or part-time modular basis for 16-19 year olds. These colleges would be run under college regulations, and managed by local, or possibly new regional, authorities. The central administration of the system would require the creation of a new Department of Education and Training, possibly divided into different authorities for training, education and Higher Education. Education and industry would need to be represented at all levels, and there might well be a case for the involvement of new regional units of administration since the interests of the economy are best represented at this rather than local levels.

Reorganization along these lines would certainly be a radical departure but it would not be a leap into the dark. In Sweden post-16 education and training is already integrated, delivered through the comprehensive Gymnasieskolan, administered by the regional authorities. The French also have an education-led system although one divided between the traditional lycées and the new vocational lycées professionnels. However, these have been moving steadily together with the broadening of the baccalauréat to include vocational subjects, and there is now a trend towards the creation of new integrated lycées polyvalents. In this country we also have a model in the tertiary colleges, now numbering over 50 and very successful, both in raising participation rates and in providing opportunities for students to study a wide variety of different general and vocational subjects in flexible combinations. Only the limits imposed by the fragmented examination system prevent them from offering a fully integrated provision.

Change to an integrated system certainly could not happen all at once. At the moment the underlying trend is towards the French binary model with a mixture of academic sixth-form colleges and predominantly vocational further education colleges, with youth training beginning to recede as young people increasingly opt for college courses. We have a long way to go before we achieve the participation levels in France, and we still lack an integrated examination structure like the Baccalauréat. However, staying-on is increasing and there is burgeoning support for a Baccalauréat style examination at 18. However, whilst things are slowly taking their course in the UK, and moving on to a more rational structure, countries like France are already looking ahead to a more comprehensive structure and yet higher levels of participation (the plan in France is for 80 per cent to study at bac level by the end of the century). In Britain we should also be planning for the next millennium. This should mean laying the foundations for a fully tertiary system now.

There would still be some resistance to a tertiary solution and much work needs to be done to build a consensus around this policy. Opposition would certainly come from some secondary teachers and from middle-class parents in inner city areas. The fears of these two groups need to be carefully examined. Teachers are understandably resistant to losing the sixth-form work which they value greatly. Many feel that the loss of this kind of work would detract from the quality of recruits into secondary schools and that the loss of the older students would also deprive schools of their beneficial influence. Some also argue that colleges cannot provide the quality of pastoral care that many young people need. Some middle-class parents in the inner cities particularly value the sixth-form college as a kind of substitute grammar school and regard tertiary colleges as being 'rough' and inferior academically.

The way to meet these objections is to ensure that the new tertiary college is not simply an expansion of the old FE college, still seen as the 'Tech' by many, but rather a new kind of institution entirely. They should draw their staff equally from schools and colleges so that neither group can fear the loss of career opportunities. The expansion of the system would in fact create many new posts. Many of the existing college buildings and resources would have to be used for the new tertiary colleges. They already in many cases have a wealth of equipment and facilities which schools do not have but it would be essential to upgrade the buildings, creating a pleasant working environment and making them suitable for students with special needs. Pastoral Care, or counselling, is already in fact very advanced in many colleges but more would need to be done to publicise this fact and to convince parents that the tertiary colleges would be safe, attractive and caring environments. Above all they would need to be committed to the highest standards in technical and academic education and convince the public of this fact. Our recommendations on the curriculum suggests some of the ways forward here.

Teachers working in secondary schools are often already demoralized by poor pay and conditions and repeated attacks on the profession. The loss of what remains of the sixth-forms might seem like a final straw. The difference might well be largely symbolic, since most secondary teachers do little sixth-form work now in any case, but it would nevertheless be felt strongly. However, this is not just a problem of 16-19 reorganization but a much more fundamental problem of the education service as a whole. The answer is not to forgo a reorganization which is in the interests of the students but rather to get to the heart of the underlying problem. There is absolutely no alternative here, if we are to achieve a high-quality education service, except to raise the pay, conditions and status of teachers to the level which befits such key members of our society.

Creating a tertiary system would undoubtedly be a gradual process involving widespread consultation and research, and a determined political effort to forge a new consensus around the issue. However, it would also require legislation. The decisions as to what organizational model should be adopted could not, in the end, be left to the local authorities since this would create endless delays and inconsistencies which would dilute the impact of reform and frustrate the intention to create a new coherence. The aim is to create a new national system, not a multitude of new local arrangements. The Government's plans (in the recent White Paper (1991): *Education and Training for the 21st Century*) to take colleges away from the LEAs and to finance them centrally through a new funding council might, paradoxically, make restructuring easier. In the short-term or under existing government policy, the move will put a blight on all planning and restructuring in the post-16 sector, making the creation of new tertiary colleges impossible, and jeopardising the nascent tertiary networks which have grown up in institutionally mixed systems through cross-institutional collaboration. It will also further fragment the system by separating LEA-controlled sixth-forms from centrally funded Colleges, creating a free-for-all amongst competing institutions. However, under a new Government, committed to reorganization, the removal of LEA control in this area would clear the path for implementing a new national structure which, once established, could be returned to local or regional control.

Higher Education

The structure of higher education also needs reform. The rationale for a binary system of universities and polytechnics is now utterly dated since they perform exactly the same function, but with unequal resources. This resource allocation now needs to be equalized. The bifurcation of control between public sector and university higher education is also anomalous and presents an important obstacle to the planned expansion and reform of the system which the country needs. Both sectors depend on public resourcing and both should be accountable to the elected representatives. The most appropriate level for such accountability would be at the level of the region. The Government is currently planning the merger of universities and polytechnics through the amalgamation of their funding bodies. However, this does not represent a new commitment to the unitary system recommended by Robbins but rather a downgrading of the majority of universities to the resource level of polytechnics. The majority of universities and polytechnics would then become teaching only institutions, run on strictly cost-benefit principles. Only a few institutes would be left to concentrate on research. Such a change would be absolutely disastrous for the research base of this country, which is already dangerously diminished after years of cuts in higher education and research and development budgets.

The precise structure of a reformed higher education system needs further consideration. It is clear, however, that it should become a unitary system where all institutions are equally concerned with research and teaching. It would be hard to overestimate the importance of institutions of higher education as facilitators of original research both pure and applied, and in the arts and sciences. If the polytechnics have a traditional bias towards applied research, and the universities to pure or open ended research, the bringing of the two together can only be beneficial. Britain's historical record in pure, 'curiosity-led' research has been outstanding, but its ability to develop the results in socially useful applications has not always been so good. By bringing the two sectors of higher education together the traditional gulf between theory and practice may be more easily bridged.

If research is a paramount concern of all institutions of higher education, then so is teaching. The highest quality of teaching at this level can be sustained only if those involved are also engaged in the research which refreshes, stimulates and advances their approach to their subjects. In recent years the polytechnics, in particular, have often demonstrated rapid responsiveness to the changing needs of their students, and a willingness to innovate in the design and planning of new courses and the development of new forms of delivery. The merger of the universities with the polytechnics would no doubt quicken the process of reform in higher education. Plans should be developed speedily for the amalgamation of these sectors into a unitary system.

Notes

1. See Stuart Maclure, *Educational Documents: England and Wales: 1816 to the present day*, London: Methuen, 1986, p.142.
2. Quoted in Clyde Chitty's Introduction to C. Chitty (ed.), *Post-Sixteen Education: Studies in Access and Achievement*, Kogan Page, 1991, p.14.
3. Stuart Sexton, *Our Schools - A Radical Policy*, The Institute of Economic Affairs, 1987, p.9.
4. See Richard Lynn's own account in *Educational Achievement in Japan*, Macmillan, 1988.
5. See Caroline Benn, 'The Public Price of Private Education and Privatization,' *Forum*, Vol. 32, No. 3, Summer 1990, pp.68-73.
6. Quoted in A.S. Bishop, *The Rise of a Central Authority for English Education*, Cambridge University Press, 1971, p.vii.
7. See Brian Simon, 'Thatcher's Third Tier, or Bribery and Corruption,' *Forum*, Vol. 32, No. 3, Summer, 1990, p.77.
8. Ibid, p.75.
9. Caroline Benn, *All Faiths in All Schools*, SEA, 1986.
10. Labour Policy Review, *Meet the Challenge. Make the Change*, The Labour Party 1989.
11. DES, *Statistical Bulletin*, 18/86, Table 1.
12. Caroline Benn, *All Faiths in All Schools*, SEA, 1986.
13. Institute for Public Policy Research (IPPR) *A British Baccalauréat: ending the division between education and training*, IPPR, 1990, p.4.

Chapter Four

The National Curriculum and Assessment: Changing Course

Clyde Chitty, Tamara Jakubowska and Ken Jones

The National Curriculum embodies a rejection of the model of educational administration that has dominated most of this century: that of a 'national system, locally administered.' This system, it is argued, was unresponsive to the needs of parents; it conceded to teachers effective power over what was taught and how it was taught. As a result, schools were slow to make necessary changes, while, in many cases, they were keen to seize on fads that were of no benefit to students.

The National Curriculum, it is claimed, will change all that. It is based on the principles of accountability and entitlement. It has been able to preserve important subjects, such as history, that were in danger of disappearance or dilution; to bring definition and order to others that, like English, had become shapeless; and to entitle all students - girls as well as boys - to study subjects like science and technology. It sets out what students should learn and allows effective measurement of their progress towards learning it. Thus - so the claim goes - it makes clear and public what were once intuitive and half-articulated judgements about curriculum content and student performance.

This is a case which needs answering. But before doing so, we need to indicate how this ideal version of the National Curriculum matches up to the reality of its implementation. The original 1987 proposals for a National Curriculum appeared to marginalize both Her Majesty's Inspectors with their plans for a curriculum based on 'areas of experience', and the so-called 'Conservative Modernizers' or 'Industrial Trainers' who were so influential while Keith Joseph was at the DES and David Young headed the MSC. Now the latter group appears to have made a comeback. The continued and growing stress on 'differentiation' is producing a system in which the concept of 'universal entitlement' has lost its initial currency; ministers now assume that, from the age of 14 onwards, students may follow either vocational or academic courses.

Changes like these, in diluting the original claims for entitlement, reduce the force of the case for the National Curriculum. It is losing whatever claim it once possessed to egalitarianism and reveals instead the place in holds in a system based on privilege, difference and - for some - self-confirming low expectations.

In these more recent developments - announced by ministers in early 1991 - there is much to criticize. But we also dispute the claims made for any 'ideal' version of the present National Curriculum: even if it didn't contain the explicit systems of differentiation now proposed, we would not support it.

So - what is our position? In an earlier chapter we argued that 'the education system in the UK is still multiply fragmented', and that this fragmentation is the basis of inequality. From this starting point, we called for a uniform system of educational provision as the only credible basis of a comprehensive system. Following the argument through, should we not now be arguing the case for a common, national curriculum as a means of promoting standardized, normative expectations that might encourage achievement among all students? Shouldn't this lead us to some qualified approval of the Conservatives' initiative?

That is not the road we are taking. We accept both the political necessity and the educational usefulness of national, broadly-stated curriculum objectives. We think that these could have a positive role in setting out the entitlement of all students, and in preventing the diversity and concomitant inequalities of curriculum provision that have marked the English education system. To state curriculum objectives of the sort we set out in a later section would encourage discussion with students and parents and would permit - indeed, encourage - curriculum initiative. But objectives of this sort, we insist, are of a quite different order to those set out in the National Curriculum: they do not seek to tie down curriculum development in so narrow a way; nor are they related to an intellectually untenable tabulation of 'levels of attainment'. In short, we are not interested in producing a left-wing version of the National Curriculum, but in rethinking the relationship between the practice of schools and the curriculum policies of governments. It is from this perspective, then, that we approach the National Curriculum and attempt to develop alternatives to it.

We begin by making a distinction between the central state's role in relation to resources and organization, and the role it claims through a National Curriculum as controller of much of the detail of the learning process. The former we see as essential to the creation of the minimum conditions for equality: guarantees of rights of access and uniformity of provision. The latter we do not view so positively. The determination of the curriculum by government will, of course, have some impact on the more backward kinds of educational practice: the Right's expressions of horror at the National Curriculum's endorsement of 'speaking and listening' as activities central to learning are a kind of perverse homage to this aspect of the modernizing process. But that is not the main point. More important for us is the deadening effect, short and long-term, that curriculum direction by the central state will have on radical educational change.

In some European countries - France is the classic example - there is a tradition, whose origins at least are revolutionary, of the state acting as destroyer of feudal, or clerical, or merely parochial backwardness; and as creator of modern and secular educational systems, whose curricula can claim to be the embodiment of rational, universalist thought. This is a powerful tradition, which has given rise to an equally powerful 'progressive' rhetoric, which links together modernization, citizenship and national unity. It is worth recalling, though, the other side of this tradition. Universality and rationality were the masks worn by an education that was systematic in its denial of the experience of subordinate classes and regional populations. The curriculum of such a system was and is highly selective in its attitude to the cultures, the interests and the social objectives of these groups. Yet it is exactly these areas which would need to be addressed by a curriculum which saw itself as helping to empower oppressed groups. Such a curriculum would aim to move between - on the one hand - issues arising from the lives of learners and - on the other - the general relationships which structured those issues and those lives. Likewise, it would move between everyday common sense and formally-organized conceptual systems. It would not centre itself on a universalism that concealed the presence of specific social interests; nor would it limit itself to a 'curriculum of everyday life', confined to the local and particular.

From this viewpoint, the inadequacies of any highly specified national curriculum are clear. Claiming its relevance to all students, it in fact neglects the specific conditions of their lives, and the interests which motivate or impede their learning; the model of knowledge which it presents to students is unlikely to be attractive.

Our arguments in favour of a predominant role for local determination of the curriculum should now, we hope, be clearer. They are essentially of two kinds. The first concerns pedagogy: effective, empowering learning demands the closest attention by educators to the cultural and social specificities of class, race and gender. It is these specificities which are ironed out by the National Curriculum. The second argument is political: it is only in such a system that space would be available for curriculum change of the sort we favour. It is only, at present, through such a system that a movement for radical curriculum development can in practice be built. To believe that it can occur via the intervention of the central state greatly overestimates what is possible - for now and the medium-term future, at least.

These, then, are the starting points from which we approach the National Curriculum implemented by the Conservative Government. Now we wish to move to a more detailed kind of criticism.

The Context of the National Curriculum
The National Curriculum is just one part of the Education 'Reform' Act. It cannot be understood without reference to others, especially open enrolment and local management of schools. In this system, schools will stand or fall according to their success in attracting students. Test results will be crucial in determining a school's success in the market. This means that tests, and the curriculum which is the basis of tests, have to be planned with a view to providing information which can be easily summarized and publicized in the form of scores, and of league tables based on these scores. Thus complex skills and understandings have to be articulated, simplistically, as performances on a scale of 1-10. In turn, this generates assessment procedures which involve great amounts of teacher time, are often extrinsic to the everyday work of students, and productive of stress for students and teachers alike.

A curriculum of this sort involves specification down to a considerable level of detail. It is an elaborately planned central initiative, packaged ready for foolproof local delivery. Yet the educational system into which this model scheme is being inserted is experiencing difficulties that arise from the lack of effective planning and resources which is as much a feature of Conservative education as is central control. The effects of this mixture of plan and planlessness can be measured in primary schools: grandiose plans are not matched by generous resources. In most areas, time in school hours for discussing and planning these changes will be non-existent. In some areas, teacher shortage makes the task more implausible still. Planning, paradoxically, deepens the difficulties of the teacher.

There is a further, related problem, stemming from the distrust of teachers, which is basic to the National Curriculum. Teachers, unavoidably, will play a great part in the implementing of curriculum change, but virtually none in its devising. As in other similar cases of deskilling, planning and execution have been separated. Much is expected; little that is creative is offered. Staffrooms, in the era of the National Curriculum, are becoming places of frantic activity and deep alienation. Top-down planning threatens to create a disenchanted teaching force. In the process, the energies for radical change that once - not so long ago - existed in some depth have been overwhelmed or diverted.

Finally, in establishing the context of the National Curriculum, it is worth adding a point about 'accountability'. For all the currency that this term has in Conservative rhetoric, parental - still less student - input into the National Curriculum is negligible. Parents have the right to complain that the National Curriculum is not being delivered; but they have no right to participate in discussions that could shape the curriculum policies of the school, in the way they might relate to local need.

The Model of the Curriculum

The National Curriculum, reflecting the thinking of the Right, is subject-centred. Despite efforts to graft on to its subject basis a number of 'cross-curricular' themes, it relates to no clear conception of what students' educational experience should comprise as a whole. It does not rest on an explicit set of objectives, and articulates no clear ideas about learning processes. Instead, objectives are worked out in a fragmented way, in relation to different subjects. No thought is given to the climate of school life as a whole, and important areas of need are not addressed in a satisfactory way. 'Equal Opportunities' is a predictable loser in this process: difference and diversity, and the opportunities and conflicts they create are missing.

Attempts to develop such areas within the National Curriculum are not only hampered by the subject-centred framework and by the interventionist hostility of the Government, but also by the weight of detail in the curriculum's programmes of study. The National Curriculum leaves little scope, or time, for experiment. It thus implicitly, as well as explicitly, discourages schools from trying to find new ways of identifying and meeting students' needs. Hasty in the way it is being implemented, the National Curriculum promises inertia once it is in place.

Built into the model of the curriculum is a model of the learner. This is implicit in frequently-repeated statements to the effect that it will be 'relevant' to all students, 'regardless of' their race, gender or class - though these over-explicit terms are usually avoided. It is difficult to see how this neglect of the cultures of students, which departs from some of the developing recognitions of teachers in the seventies and eighties, can develop a meaningful education, or raise significantly levels of achievement.

In its basic shape, then, and in its attitude to the active role of teachers and students, the National Curriculum reflects traditionalist conceptions. These are probably the most important effects of right-wing thinking on the curriculum. But there are others: the treatment of the languages of minorities (except Welsh); the complacent treatment of Britain's imperial history; the deliberate failure to give science a satisfactory social context. In addition, the legislative successes of the Right in relation to issues such as 'political partisanship' in teaching, and the presentation of questions of 'homosexuality', have had a considerable effect in deterring particular kinds of educational initiative.

In these largely negative ways the Right has imposed its pressure on the new system. But this does not mean that what is specified in each individual subject area conforms to right-wing thinking. In many respects - the activity-based nature of testing, the importance of oral work and of investigation, the departure from ideas of a literary canon - the influence of more progressive currents can be detected. Developments of this sort have been important in involving a large section of educationalists in the National Curriculum. Many, acting from a desire to make the new curriculum as acceptable as possible, have followed a policy of 'constructive engagement'. This strategy has succeeded in defending and even in developing some good practice, but it has been followed at the expense of a larger vision of educational purpose.

Testing

Perhaps the most depressing sentence in the 1987 DES consultation document *The National Curriculum 5-16* told us that 'at the heart of the assessment process, there will be nationally prescribed tests, done by all students to supplement the individual teachers' assessments.' It was envisaged in 1987 that attainment targets would be set for the three core subjects of maths, English and science and for the 'foundation' subjects where appropriate. These targets would provide standards against which students' progress and performance could be assessed. Much of the assessment at ages 7, 11 and 14, and at 16 in non-examined subjects, would be carried out by teachers as an integral part of normal classroom work. But there would be a key role for the nationally prescribed tests, administered and marked by teachers, with their marking - and their assessments overall - externally moderated. These tests and other forms of assessment would be developed and piloted by various organizations on behalf of the government. In the meantime, the precise basis for recording assessments would be considered by an expert Task Group on Assessment and Testing to be appointed by the Secretary of State.

It was originally assumed by the (then) Prime Minister's Far Right advisers - and indeed by the Prime Minister herself - that the new tests would be simple 'pencil and paper' affairs, along the lines we associate with the largely defunct 11-plus. The Centre for Policy Studies, which has had close links with Downing Street, believed that effective testing involved the development of formal, simple, external and standardized procedures. The 1988 CPS document *Correct Core: Simple Curricula for English Maths and Science* contains examples of what around 85 per cent of children ought to be able to do by the ages of 7, 11, 14 and 16.

But the TGAT proposals were far more sophisticated than anything envisaged by the far right. The two major surprises were the now-famous SATs (Standard Assessment Tasks) and the system of 'levels of attainment'. The tasks were meant to be sufficiently wide-ranging to avoid curricular distortion; and the levels were designed to allow for differentiation, variation and progression. We know from the leaked letter from the Prime Minister's Office, dated 21 January 1988, that Mrs. Thatcher was profoundly unhappy with the TGAT proposals. She had always wanted traditional tests, rather than an assessment system which validated aspects of 'progressive' practice - such as group work - and which placed a heavy responsibility on teachers' judgements.

The battle between traditionalists and the TGAT approach is not over yet, and is still being waged in the guise of a dispute over the complexity of assessment procedures. Yet it is important not to get too enthusiastic about the 'progressive' nature of the TGAT framework. The National Curriculum's assessment system rests on a number of sets of 'levels of attainment', which seeks to define a step-by-step ladder of intellectual development in different aspects of each subject. It is important to question the validity of this model of development; it is linear, whereas learning is not; it assigns particular skills to particular levels of attainment in arbitrary ways; it lays claim to a scientific objectivity which will obscure the social nature of many learning activities; and in its repeated, long-drawn-out and public nature it will confirm the sense of failure of many, and re-install competition as a central feature of all stages of education. The recommendations are essentially a compromise - appearing to find a role for professional expertise, while at the same time they give civil servants and politicians the kind of information they need for accountability, control and the efficient running of a market system of schools. Students' scores can be aggregated to show results for a class, a school and even a whole LEA for comparative purposes; and this is the sort of information parents can use to make superficial judgements about the desirability or otherwise of individual schools.

Teachers soon discovered that the TGAT proposals were costly, cumbersome and time-consuming. For example, maths, science and English involved 32 'attainment targets' for Key Stage one alone. There were to be 227 'statements of attainment' for maths, science and English, which meant that for a class of thirty seven-year-olds, a teacher would need to grapple with as many as 6810 statements of attainment. By the end of 1990, the government was having to modify its original demands - deciding, for example, that the tests at the end of Key Stage One should cover only nine attainment targets instead of the original 32. Even so, the 'SAT' procedures of 1991 proved deeply controversial. It was not only problems of teacher workload that were highlighted, nor even the disruption to useful education caused by the SAT procedures. It was also the case that the weaknesses of National Curriculum assessment as a whole were shown up: what the tests measured was not what teachers considered best practice; the claim that they provided objective, standardized information about students' capabilities was weakened by the evident disparities in staffing and resourcing between different schools and even between different classes in the same school.

What could be the future of testing? From the Right, there has continued to come demands for 'simple' pencil and paper tests; and Prime Minister John Major appeared to endorse this approach in a speech to the right-wing Centre for Policy Studies on 3 July 1991. It is plainly inadequate to oppose these tests in the name of defending the current system. It is necessary instead to develop alternatives both to the Right and to the TGAT model. In this respect, it is important to emphasize the distinction between diagnostic testing, which is primarily school-based and enables teachers to discover the strengths and weaknesses of their students, and the sorts of testing advocated by the Government, which focuses narrowly upon outcomes, rather than performance, and is concerned chiefly with superficial comparison, not only between students, but also between teachers and between schools. Teachers do not need SATs - nor the criteria established by the National Curriculum for continuous teacher assessment - to tell them how their students are performing. They do need to develop the kind of work that went into the ILEA's *Primary Language Record* - a model for the kind of assessment, based on teacher observation, which demands of teachers that they use and develop their knowledge of language in ways that allow them to identify and work with the strengths and weaknesses of students. The *Primary Language Record* asks teachers to write their personal observations of students' work, using criteria of progress derived from extensive discussion and consultation. It asks them to discuss these observations with students and with their parents, and to make them available to those who have an educational interest in them. All this - expressed, as one of its devisers put it, in words not the crude numbers which are the products of SATs - is a far cry from the National

Curriculum. It suggests the possibility of an assessment system based on a national system of formative Records of Achievement, based in part upon the involvement of students in the evaluation of their own learning. In the long term, such a system might well remove the necessity for a 'school-leaving' exam at 16. As the recent IPPR document *A British Baccalauréat* points out, 'Britain is unique among Western countries in the importance it attaches to a public, "school-leaving" exam at 16.' Such a qualification says much about our obsession in this country with the idea that learning should be interrupted by a series of hurdles to further advance. The GCSE would in any case be redundant if participation to 18 became the norm.

An Alternative Curriculum

Some General Principles
The criticisms of the National Curriculum outlined thus far do not mean, however, that we depart from the concept of a nationally-agreed statement of a common curriculum. The latter would be important in generating democratic discussion involving educationalists, parents, students, unions, employers and community representatives about the aims and principles of education, and in laying the basis for the minimum entitlement to education of all students. A statement of entitlement to a common curriculum would commit central government to a better resourcing of education and would help to prevent the inequalities created by wide differentiation in provision - in the past, for instance, comprehensive schools have not made the same quality of curriculum offer to all students.

An alternative policy would need to develop a curriculum which was neither the 'secret garden' of the professionals as in the past, nor the present centrally-imposed one. It would need to be based on a nationally-agreed statement of entitlement arrived at through wide debate, but be flexible enough to be elaborated upon by educationalists, students, parents and community groups at a local level, to meet local needs. There would need to be a balance within the curriculum between the needs, aspirations and interests of the individual student, and the needs of the community and wider world.

Access to knowledge, skills and understanding should not just occur through compartmentalized subject areas. Students should be offered the opportunity to see the links between areas of knowledge, and to develop and transfer skills and concepts from one area to another. The traditional structuring of knowledge and knowledge acquisition should be broken down: for example, the divisions between 'mental' and 'manual' skills, 'academic' and 'vocational', 'theory' and 'practice', 'experts' and 'lay' people. The curriculum should enable students to study science and technology not just in their technical aspects, but also in relation to social and ecological questions. In later years, vocational preparation should train students not just in the skills and information necessary for the world of work, but also in the ability to scrutinize it critically and change the situation in which they find themselves according to their developing aspirations.

To ensure that all students achieve their full potential, the curriculum - both formal and hidden - should actively discourage inequalities of access *and* outcome on the basis of class, race, sex, sexuality and disability. The curriculum should be secular in its orientation but should value and take account of the cultures, language, skills and experiences that students bring with them.

With regard to students with special educational needs, the principle established in the 1981 Education Act - that, as far as is practicable, such students should be educated in ordinary schools - should be adhered to. It should be recognized, however, that in order to achieve successful integration and ensure that the special educational needs of students in making optimum progress within a mainstream curriculum are fully met, schools must be adequately resourced. Again, one of the functions of a nationally-agreed statement of entitlement would be that the state at central level would be responsible for resourcing such provision.

The curriculum should be delivered in a forum that allows academic freedom: the ability to discuss and debate freely, together with safeguards for those who hold views that go against prevailing orthodoxies. Within such a forum, students should be entitled to learn about a variety of values and perspectives. The curriculum should promote the ability of students to conceptualize, theorize, evaluate critically, communicate easily, make informed decisions, and, where necessary, help promote change.

Organization of the Curriculum

The National Curriculum would be replaced by a common curriculum to which all students, whatever their class, sex, race or ability, would be entitled. The organising principles of such a curriculum - its aims and objectives, the articulation of the essential skills, knowledge and values that it should develop - together with a common core of studies which all students should experience, could be agreed at a national level through wide and democratic debate. Such a core would not necessarily be defined within traditional subject boundaries, which may often act as a barrier to achieving the wider aims and objectives of the curriculum. The area of the literary, for example, has conventionally been offered on the curriculum as *English* literature and has been based to a large extent on the study of the traditional canon of 'great works'. As these texts have mostly achieved 'greatness' through being judged by Eurocentric or abstract notions of excellence, large areas of writing including that of - for example - women and black people have invariably been excluded. Thus the traditional study of literature has not only failed to motivate many students through the narrowness of its focus, but has thrown away the opportunity of studying works that may well help to promote a more critical awareness of the texts in the traditional canon.

The common core could offer access to knowledge based instead on areas of experience and learning such as those outlined in the three HMI 'Red Books' of 1977, 1981 and 1983 or the NUT's 1990 document *A Strategy for the Curriculum.* The latter document suggests that the curriculum should cover each of the following areas:

* aesthetic and creative
* human, social and political
* linguistic and literary
* mathematical
* moral and spiritual
* physical
* ecological, scientific and technological

The National Curriculum Statement would need to give scope for local initiative and decision-making. It would need to be flexible enough to be developed and changed in response to community needs, abilities and interests. At a local level, there should be student, parent and

community involvement in determining the content of the curriculum and in ensuring that it:
* covers the areas of experience
* meets the teaching and learning objectives of the national statement
* meets local needs
* meets student needs

An essential part of this form of curriculum development would be the encouragement of local curriculum initiatives and experimentation.

But a statement of the curriculum to which all students are entitled is no guarantee that all students will gain equal access to it: teachers need to develop programmes to ensure equality of opportunity. The curriculum should be flexible enough - for example - to allow the full participation of students with special needs. In order to avoid the danger of such students feeling unable to achieve fully in the curriculum, appropriate teaching strategies would need to be developed and adequate resources made available - both in the form of materials, and of specialist support teachers.

Through the curriculum, teachers should be actively engaged in opposing inequality on the basis of class, race, sex and sexuality. At the level of the formal curriculum there needs to be a fundamental re-appraisal of the values and assumptions that permeate and frame the way that subjects are offered in English schools. Many curriculum areas have 'naturalized' their subject matter so that what is actually based on contentious assumption - that there are no great black or women scientists, for instance - is made to seem like common sense. The curriculum, formal and hidden, needs to address itself to redressing past bias and stereotyping, to presenting positive images of traditionally disadvantaged groups, and to offering opportunities for students to develop the ability to be critical for themselves of the institutions, values and assumptions that help perpetuate inequality. It needs to be based on the recognition that successful learning takes place when the skills, experience, cultural and linguistic diversity that students bring with them to school are acknowledged and developed.

Post-16

Reforming the curriculum and assessment system post-16 is one of the most urgent tasks facing education today. The current muddled and fragmentary provision for the age group, involving multiple incompatible tracks, outmoded curricula and an incomprehensible profusion of qualifications and awarding bodies, is one of the major reasons for the low rates of participation in post-compulsory education and training. Young people often do not understand what is on offer, and where they do they often consider it inappropriate to their needs or 'not worth the trouble'. 'A' levels were not designed for the majority and have little appeal to most 16-year-olds, and vocational qualifications often appear to lack prestige and/or sufficient credibility in the labour market to warrant forfeiting an early wage to obtain. There are few opportunities to combine the two, and arrangements for progression and transfer are poor.

Recent attempts to reform curriculum and assessment post-16 have been faltering. The 1988 Higginson Report criticized A levels for being narrow, over-specialized and elitist, and recommended a shift to a broader 5-subject 'A' level model. The proposal won widespread support from a host of bodies, including BP and the CBI. However, the Government rejected the recommendations in order to maintain the 'A' level 'gold standard' - oblivious that the only value of gold lies in its scarcity value. Their alternative strategy was to introduce new A/S levels, and , more recently, to ask the National Curriculum Council to find ways of developing 'core skills' at A level. However, A/S levels have not really caught on and the core skills initiative is being quietly buried, again for fear that it might dilute the much vaunted 'A' level. What remains of the Government's strategy is to enhance vocational qualifications through the rationalization of awards promoted by the National Council for Vocational Qualifications (NCVQ) and the recent proposal to create a new tier of broader vocational qualifications to be known as GNVQs. But it is unlikely that genuine breadth can be introduced into vocational qualifications so long as the NCVQ's criterion for assessment remains the demonstration of competence directly relevant to narrowly defined job requirements. With 'A' levels unreformed it is also hard to see how the prestige of vocational qualifications can be raised and/or how academic and vocational areas of the curriculum can effectively be brought together. The White Papers of mid-1991 address, but do not resolve, this issue. Although bringing about some rationalisation of curricula and qualifications, they leave in place a system based on the two poles of academic and vocational. Pledges that each will be valued equally ring hollow.

Rather than prolonging the essentially piecemeal nature of these approaches, a much more radical reform of both the curriculum and assessment system is needed. At the basis of a new system would be some form of 'core studies', that would ensure continuity with pre-16 education, and incorporate 'vocational' and 'academic' approaches. The core might include study skills, mathematics and science, language work, media education, environmental education, arts and physical education, and education in democratic decision-making. Curricula could be developed in these areas which made use of the opportunities provided by work experience and work observation, but should also subject the world of work to the kinds of questioning that would be focused through academic disciplines. One promising idea (from the Institute of Public Policy Research) that embodies such an approach would involve the replacement of existing qualifications for the age group by a new Advanced Diploma. This would be delivered on a modular basis and assessed through credit accumulation. There would be three 'domains' of study: Social and Human Science; Natural Sciences and Technology; and Languages and Literature. In each domain there would be three types of module - designated Core, Specialist and Work/ Community-based respectively. Core and Specialist modules would include some with a more applied or practical focus and Work/ Community modules would involve structured work experience. To encourage breadth and a mix of the academic and the vocational all students would have to complete core modules of both 'theoretical' and 'applied' focus in each domain and all students would have to complete at least one work/community-based module. The assumption of the proposal is that the majority of students would attend on a full-time basis, but part-time study would be possible and students' employment experience could be assessed as part of the diploma. Assessment would be conducted internally according to clear criteria of achievement, with graded levels for each module, but there would need to be a much-strengthened system of external moderation to ensure consistency of standards.

The advantages of this model in terms of increasing choice and breadth in post-16 education and training are manifest; if provision were to be organized on a basis like this, many more young people might stay on. However, its success would entail much more than changing courses and delivery strategies. The entire examination and assessment system would have to be overhauled. This would not be possible, clearly, with the existing 300-plus awarding bodies playing their current roles. A new national council for 16-19 curricula would need to be established, with genuinely representative membership and the obligation to consult widely. It would need to be supplemented by similar bodies at the regional level, which would take into account local labour market and community needs. However, the qualifications awarded should be national, their credibility vouchsafed not by private awarding bodies but by the state - as is the case everywhere else in Europe.

Organizing learning
The organisation of learning, and of schools themselves, needs to match up with the aims of the curriculum. Schools should, for example, be democratic institutions involving all sections of their community - including students - in a discussion about the content and process of the education on offer.

The delivery of a curriculum based on democratic principles would of necessity mean the abandonment of practices such as banding and setting on the basis of 'ability'. Students should learn in flexible groupings, and not necessarily be confined to the same groups for long periods. Some of the best practice of unstreamed teaching - which recognises that within a single class it is both possible and desirable to accommodate different rates and styles of learning - would need to be adopted and developed. Such practice would necessitate teachers trained in the skills of identifying individual differences in students and responding to them by adapting the curriculum and the learning process to their specific needs. Such practice would involve less didactic delivery of the curriculum by teachers, and more activity-based, investigative and creative work. In addition to the promotion of independent learning by students, there should be maximum opportunities for collaborative learning, with teachers and students working alongside each other. In sum, such practice would enable all students to be actively involved in developing their own potential, would avoid learning situations that deemed large numbers of them failures, and would encourage achievement for all students through a stimulating and supportive, rather than competitive environment.

Chapter Five

Education for Work

Pat Ainley

Education for work is still anathema to many progressive and socialist parents and teachers despite (or perhaps because of) successive governments relentlessly advocating the concept since at least 1976. For many progressive people education is, by definition, non-vocational and concerned only with broadening the mind and developing character. For many Socialists, education for work under capitalism is a form of indoctrination for exploitation. For them the role of education is to sustain and develop a critical consciousness. Yet it was Marx and Engels who demanded that education should be combined with productive labour and who saw in the factory system of the time the prototype of schools for the future. They advocated this not only as a practical policy but also as a theoretical prescription - education cannot be understood separately from work in the society for which it directly or indirectly prepares its students. In this sense all education is vocational and should be recognized as such.

Of course ideas are also crucial to education. Investigation, experiment and argument develop new ideas from experience in order to comprehend and deal with changing reality. Today this is vital when so many received ideas in the social and natural sciences are open to question from the new perspectives opened up by accelerating historical and even climatic change. In addition new technology can be applied at every level of education to facilitate learning and allow imagination free reign beyond the immediate necessity to earn a wage and the constraints of production for profit. Indeed, it was Mrs. Thatcher herself who told the Parliamentary and Scientific Committee's 50th anniversary celebration: 'The greatest economic benefits of scientific research have always resulted from advances in fundamental knowledge rather than the search for specific applications.' This space within education for seeding new ideas must be preserved and extended.

However education is not just concerned with ideas, as learning is not restricted to acquiring book knowledge. Practical skills are equally important and are in fact the foundation of abstract conceptions. Nor can learning be limited to a reduced age range within educational institutions. In a period of rapid social change, everyone now pays lip service to the old Chinese slogan 'Life is an education and society is a school.' However, institutional arrangements have to be created to facilitate instead of, as at present, hinder lifelong learning.

If education is to be recognised as a process that involves everybody throughout their lives it must take as its starting point the skills and knowledge that enable society to produce and reproduce. People are already skilled and these skills are embodied in cultural forms that allow their transmission between generations. These skills of productive life are not limited to the workplace or to paid labour but at the workplace it is workers who train workers, not employers or 'industry.' It is only in dialogue with this existing practical knowledge that artistic and scientific knowledge can be developed to contribute to the social reconstruction of society necessary to save it from economic stagnation and ecological catastrophe. This relates to a democratic practice which expresses the ideas of the oppressed. However unsystematized these ideas are initially, they are more accurately realistic than conceptions that have been created only theoretically.

Education is therefore for collective cooperation not individual competition. The goal of education policy can no longer be the attempt made by social democracy in the past to equalize the starting points of individuals so that they can compete on equal terms for unequal places in the employment hierarchy. Nor can it be, as it was during education's vocational phase from 1976 to 1987, to fuel the competition between national capitals in a destructive and exploitative race for economic supremacy between rival imperialisms. Rhetoric about Britain becoming a 'high-productivity, high-skilled economy' involves, as the Employment Secretary, Norman Fowler said, 'leaving labour-intensive, unskilled work to others' (Speech to the Bow Group, 23 October 1989). This, and the language of 'competition' catching up with Japan/Germany etc., used for instance by the Institute for Public Policy Research in their otherwise excellent Education and Training Papers, is not the language Socialists or environmentalists can espouse. As is widely recognized, international cooperation will be essential to ensure future human survival. Particularly, new non-exploitative relations of trade and economic cooperation are necessary with the underdeveloped countries. These goals of the economic modernization to which education is to contribute must be made explicit.

Similarly, education for work cannot be limited to acquiring the technical skills and knowledge necessary for existing industrial or professional tasks. If education is to build the skills and knowledge base of society to take fullest advantage of the latest developments in technology, it must begin by recognizing how new technology has been applied during the economic restructuring of the last decade and more to deskill many tasks involved in production, distribution and services. Much of the talk about 'skill' in recent years has been a cover for creating a semi-skilled, semi-employed mass of low-paid, casual workers to be used as demand dictates.

Instead of new divisions within the working population, or the rigid traditional divisions between skilled and unskilled labour, new technology has the potential to enable the workforce to become multi-skilled and flexible in a true sense, able to apply itself across a wide range of practical and theoretical tasks, including government and management. By not only simplifying tasks but sharing and integrating them, new technology can contribute to increasing productivity with less laborious and repetitive effort. It thus presents an historic opportunity for overcoming the ancient division between workers by hand and those by brain. This challenges the hierarchy of white over blue collar workers, of office over plant, managers over managed and those who think over those who do. This is certainly the logic of technical evolution and it is one that should be used to unite employees who have been divided in other ways (through age, gender, housing, education, etc.) and to isolate those few who really control and own the means of production and who benefit directly (as opposed to indirectly) from the imperialist system that is the root cause of the deepening economic, social and environmental crisis worldwide. This crisis will impose changes upon society as far-reaching as those of the last 'national emergency' during the Second World War. This time however no society can hope to survive the challenge alone and the development of technology in the industrialised countries will have to be expanded and adapted to facilitate the technological transfer necessary to literally save humanity. Despite the mass media's slavish endorsement of Britain's part in playing second fiddle to American enthusiasm for exploiting the Third World, this is becoming popularly understood.

A truly multi-skilled workforce can be only developed from the bottom up and as a result of a popular liberation, just as people have to educate themselves and cannot be forced to learn. However as a start, the state should establish the principle of a general academic and vocational education up to and beyond the age of 18. This will require legislation to provide the guidelines for developing and approving the new arrangements. Government must also establish the economic context of education-training by reaffirming the goal of full employment which was surreptitiously dropped by the last Labour Government and then explicitly abandoned by the Thatcher regime.

One lesson of the accidental boom upon which the economy stumbled in 1986 is that vocational education and regional and equal opportunities programmes all rely for their success on a well functioning national economy and labour market. They can only complement economic recovery not substitute for it. Moreover the deficit model of many special measures targeted on 'disadvantaged' (i.e. discriminated against) young people, long-term unemployed, women, ethnic minorities and the disabled has been shown to be false by the faster rate at which many of these same people took up such job opportunities as became available during the partial recovery from 1982-1988. This does not imply that training, retraining and equal opportunities policies are unnecessary, just that the primary emphasis should always be upon sustaining a balanced economic development.

It is becoming increasingly clear that the Thatcher Government in their alliance with moribund finance capital had no real interest in any such development of what remains of productive industrial capital. Major's policy of deliberately driving the economy into recession in order to protect City speculators (until Saddam Hussein managed it far more spectacularly for him) was at complete variance with any attempt to modernize and regenerate British industry. Meanwhile the policy of enterprise and the effort to engender competition in every area of national life can only hamper the co-ordination of industry with its infrastructure that is required. This moribund market modernization is more concerned with exacerbating social divisions and so maintaining the grasp of the ruling class than with any industrial strategy. For education certainly the emphasis upon competition to raise 'standards' serves mainly to widen social divisions and foster an irrelevant and academic 'national' curriculum. This rehashed version of the 1904 grammar-school curriculum does not even pretend any longer to address the problem of education for work.

In place of the moribund market modernization supported only by academic ideology embodied in the 1988 Act, there is the potential for an alliance between industrial capital and a future government that would attempt a competitive modernization of British industry. Even though this attempt to compete more effectively with rival imperialist countries would inevitably fail, in its context advances could be made towards a more open, relevant and less hierarchical education and training system. Education and training policy should be seen as part of such a wider industrial strategy but Socialists and ecologists will clearly have their own agenda within it. Initially however there could be an identity of interest between the proponents of this modernization and the modernization from the bottom up which is required for real Socialist and environmental progress. All parties could agree that the first task must be to rescue state education from chaos and its second-class status to private schooling.

The first priority for any government seriously committed to any real modernization is to re-establish the purpose of education, science and the arts in society: to stimulate thought and develop new knowledge and skills to deal with a rapidly changing situation. In the words of the 1990 NUT document *A Strategy for the Curriculum* , 'The love of learning, the ability to learn and the confidence to learn must be the central objectives of schools' (p.1). It is easy to say that education should be about liberation but it is vital to establish this as a goal of policy because it is the contradiction between education's liberatory promise and its repressive and selective practice that is at the root of so much disenchantment with schooling as it is (especially secondary schooling where the selective pressures for future employment are most acute).

Amongst the essential aims for a reforming government to make clear are:

1. The normality and desirability of full-time education for all to 18 and of recurring returns to learning full- and part-time thereafter for as many people as possible. The normality of leaving general and usually full-time education/training at 18 should also be used to emphasise the assumption of full citizenship rights and responsibilities from age 18 - not 25, as is increasingly the case. School/college leaving 'proms' at 18 could be used to make this point and would be well received since they are widely understood by young people brought up on American culture. Financial support should be available to students from the age of 16 onwards through Social Security (means related) in order to raise participation rates and the rate of return post-18. The Government has set admirable targets for increasing numbers in higher education but contradicted them by introducing loans to pay for courses raised to their full cost. Predictably loans will only restrict access to HE. They must be abolished and the recommendation of the 1963 Robbins Report re-established of access to HE for all who can benefit from it. Similarly, proposals for and experiments with credit or voucher schemes for FE and youth training can be seen only as pioneering this unworkable brainchild of the free-market right across the whole education system.

2. The duty of employers to provide training to agreed standards for anyone under 18 whom they employ and workers' entitlement to paid day-release and sabbaticals to education-training. The Confederation of British Industry has already proposed in *Towards A Skills Revolution* that no one under 18 should be employed without the integration of continuing education and training in their work. But the onus should be on employers to pay for this, not on young people to find training or pay for it through credits. This should prevent employers, especially the small employers who are the main culprits, from encouraging young people to leave school at the earliest opportunity. Access to training for 'good' jobs 'with prospects' must remain open beyond 16. This is the single most effective way of ensuring more young people remain in full-time education and do not leave at 16 in hopes of getting one of the few remaining skilled jobs still available locally. Staying on rates for females have already risen beyond 50 per cent due to young women remaining in school or going to college to obtain the further qualifications

necessary for them to gain access to many office jobs. The Youth Training Scheme however only sustained and aggravated the antique apprentice-boy model of training. This is inappropriate to industry that is no longer so labour intensive and that has a rapid rate of technological change.

3. Abolition of Youth Training which, along with Employment Training and other 'workfare' schemes, has become totally discredited by its association with unemployment relief. Restoration of social security rights to those under 18 for whom there is as yet no work and who do not wish to remain in full-time education after 16. The right to work must be reasserted as well as the 'right to training', which has been substituted for it but is often not training at all, i.e. the right to work with training. Training without jobs is rightly perceived as pointless; if employers cannot actually guarantee employment after training and the trainee to remain for a period with the employer, as in the old articles of apprenticeship, training must be to standards which are at least credible in local labour markets. Minimum wages and protective labour legislation for young workers should also be reinstated.

For those in and out of employment tertiary/further/adult colleges are well placed to become the lynch-pin of the new system, encouraging progression from schools and adult education and facilitating access to higher education. Before the government cut the colleges loose into the market place in order to bail itself out of the poll tax grave it had dug for itself, FE colleges had already begun to integrate with higher education through Open College arrangements and other flexible forms of access which are being piloted in many institutions. FE colleges are also well integrated with what remains of skill training in local labour markets and and through TVEI and other 'bridging' arrangements with their local secondary and special schools they have begun to link up with 14-18 year old school students. Many argue, of course, that the best model for the provision of post-16 education and training is the tertiary college.

Unity and agreement between the various teaching unions in the schools, further, higher and adult sectors will be required for this co-operation. Ideally all teachers/lecturers will one day be included within one union. Together with an increase in all education staff's (not just teachers/lecturers') pay, as an immediate statement of intent and priority by a new government, interchangeability between staff at different levels of education and with trainers at work will do much to raise the status of teachers. However cultural as well as practical problems have to be overcome - the English distinction between school and college, which does not exist elsewhere, e.g. the USA, where everyone from professors to infant teachers 'teaches school.'

As to the means of education and training to 18: the principle of modularized and non-academic A levels for all students is now widely accepted, and advocated for example by the Institute for Public Policy Research. Instead of 'cramming' for entry to higher education, the methods of learning and assessment associated with GCSE should be raised by teachers/lecturers from the schools through to the tertiary/FE colleges with continuous assessment and self-assessment contributing to a New Advanced Diploma.

As to content, as the IPPR says, 'economic progress demands that learning imbue work, and not vice versa' (p.22). However their unrealistic expectations of a harmony between 'education-for-work' and 'education-for-fulfilment' could lead to a curriculum dedicated to the overall needs of industry. These 'needs' have more to do with productivity and work intensification than with breaking down fundamental divisions between the managers and the managed. The 'needs' of industry have to be set in a wider framework of human and environmental need. To do this requires a greater theoretical contribution to work-related education and training. In particular, relating theory to the specific life experiences of students and trainees - 'work experience' in a deeper sense than it is habitually used. From this starting point an anti-imperialist curriculum must lead to understanding of the organization of the economy as a whole and to the relationships of power and possession that are involved in it. It will insist on international connections, on understanding 'domestic' as well as paid employment and on considering ecological consequences.

In a modular system, it will be vital not to lose sight of the divisions between disciplines as well as the inter-relations between them. It is important to distinguish between 'genuine' fields of study and practice corresponding to defined areas of reality on the one hand, and on the other, outdated academic subject divisions, as for example in the 'national' curriculum, which only hinder thought and dampen discovery.

Whilst advances in knowledge often come from the imaginative projection from one frame of reference to another, this is not the same as a 'pick-n-mix' of modules from different areas of study. Guided only by vocational (i.e. labour market) choice, there is a loss of theoretical abstraction in favour of practical application to occupational tasks not conceptually related to one another. At another level, modular higher education could also encourage the tendency towards 'educational consumerism' evident in some universities, where middle class students take 'interesting' and 'exciting' courses for the cultural cachet. Philosophical discussion, counselling and support is required if the modular method is not to degenerate into a way of just packing in and processing more students, as it already has in some polytechnics.

To ensure that the modular Advanced Diploma, while it is employment-related, is not employment-led, educational interests must have more influence in the National Council for Vocational Qualifications, if it is retained, and especially if it is to extend its remit beyond the NVQ level 3 to NVQ levels 4 and 5 equivalent to diploma and degree level professional/managerial qualifications. The NCVQ should also be linked to Workplace Training Committees, as recommended by the Trades Union Congress. These will monitor standards from level (1), general preparatory qualifications, through craft level (2), to technician (3), and supervisory (4), managerial (5). They will be made up of employee and employer representatives and have powers of co-determination with employers within enterprises, as already exist in Germany. Powers of co-determination can be raised at different levels and stages of social ownership. In the meantime and initially, WTCs can begin by conducting 'training audits' in their workplaces in the same way people are now talking about registering environmental concerns. Such audits will be the basis upon which to develop internal training within enterprises, opening opportunities to all sections of the workforce and fostering a training culture by workers themselves training the trainees on the German Meister model. As in Germany, no firm over a given size should be able to trade without a qualified worker-trainer to every so many trainees at lower levels. In addition, worker-trainerships will help to provide a career ladder based upon skills in industry. Firms can be encouraged to train young workers and retrain returnees in-house by grants and there will have to be a training levy on employers per employee whether they train them or not.

This reinstated levy-grant system will be nationally set while locally administered at the level of local labour markets. Vocational education must be rescued from the market place, where it will always be low on employers' priorities. Instead of self-appointed little groups of local businessmen (almost invariably) on Training and Enterprise Councils, all public expenditure on education and training must be publicly reported and accounted for directly to democratically elected bodies. These will in most cases be the education-training committees of local education authorities, though in some cases where the local labour market does not coincide with LEA boundaries they will have to be wider-ranging and drawn from a larger franchise, for example: all-London rather than local borough. They will also have a vital role to play in regional regeneration and will therefore have to relate to any regionally constituted representative organizations.

A new Ministry of Education and Training will establish the national framework for this innovation, whilst setting and monitoring national/ European standards. To do this it will have to be very different from today's DES that is so enthusiastically implementing the academic and centralist measures of the Conservative Government. Nor can it be the Super-Ministry for Education and Training which was Lord Young's aspiration for the Manpower Services Commission. While such a ministry may exist (along with rejigged Ministries of Employment/ Labour, Health separated from Social Security, etc.), the control of education and training must remain in the hands of the workforce and be locally democratically accountable.

Democratic control of schools and colleges, as of other public institutions, by the people involved must be reasserted over the accountability through the market which 'free-market' philosophies advocate as the most efficient method of public accountability, increasingly substituting market mechanisms for democratic accountability. (The logic of this argument is that a 'free market' is more democratic than any form of democracy and that free markets are the essence of democracy. For that reason vast multi-national bureaucratic corporations do not need to be made democratically accountable for the decisions which they afflict upon, literally, billions of people, because they have already been endorsed by the mandate of the market. Local councils, education and health authorities, on the other hand, have to be made 'more accountable', and less democratic, by converting their services into commodities which can be quantified so as to compete in an open market of 'free' consumer choice. This argument must be turned on its head.)

In the depressed regions and the inner cities education-training can be developed around the economic and social regeneration of the locality, with rebuilding programmes on the most run-down estates, for example, being used to develop building skills and knowledge under the control of and using the personal resources and experience of the residents. The general principle of giving most to those who have least will apply here as well as to the most deprived schools and colleges to compensate for educational selection by residence. This will reverse the present Biblical priorities of giving to them that already hath.

There will clearly be a redirection of resources, away from specialized and elitist institutions such as the City Technology Colleges. These are widely recognized as expensive irrelevancies and have been condemned by most leading industrialists. At the time of their launch by Mr. Baker in 1986, they had more to do with providing a model for running schools which opted out of local authority control than with answering Britain's training needs. They were also an admission that the previous policy of trying to bring vocational education to all schools had failed due to lack of the private funding that had been promised. The Baker's dozen of these schools that may soon exist can easily be reabsorbed into their LEAs to service IT training in their neighbouring industry, colleges and the schools whence their pupils and teachers may return. For it would cost £3 billion to equip every secondary school in the country to the standard of the first CTC in Solihull (a fraction of the cost of the Trident missile system but still a sum no future government is likely to invest in education).

Instead of following the CTC model of putting all your computers in one basket, the example provided by Education 2000 in Letchworth and elsewhere shows how communities can commit themselves to computer literacy for the new industrial revolution. The Letchworth project began with meetings where young people were encouraged to define their own educational needs in line with the aim of allowing people to take responsibility for their own learning. One of the striking findings to emerge at this preliminary stage was that young people, while they want recognition of their own particular needs, do not always necessarily want separate facilities from adults but often prefer integration with them. The series of discussions culminated in the adoption of a mission statement defining the new pre-vocational skills which education undertook to help provide for the town's citizens. These included 'the ability to feel comfortable amidst all the changes of a highly technological democratic society - to think, communicate, collaborate and make decisions.'

Computers are a tool to achieve this goal and the six Letchworth secondary schools have them in all departments at a ratio of one computer to every ten students. Within five years they hope to have one lap-top for every student at a cost of £2 million. Similarly, Hampshire, one of the largest English education authorities, planned before the latest government cuts to give every student in its 114 secondary schools and sixth-form colleges access to modern computing systems at a cost of £10 million over five years, with a further £5 million for its junior schools, just £3 million extra spending per year to reach the ratio of one computer to eight students.

Professor Tom Stonier of Bradford University's Department of Science and Society has calculated the costs of providing all children in Britain with a computer system to be used at home and at school. 'If spread over a six-year period, this would run to approximately £500 million a year or five per cent of the present education budget. As a result the country would become truly computerate, for you would be getting equipment into the vast majority of homes. The amount of commercial activity generated in terms of hardware and software production, servicing, training, etc., would provide a further instructive stimulus to the economy and create the kind of intellectual infrastructure to assure a technologically literate society in the next century.'

The release of facilities in schools and colleges caused by the demographic drop in the numbers of teenagers creates opportunities for providing education and training for the 70 per cent of the current workforce who have not acquired any worthwhile vocational qualification, as well as the three million people unemployed. With investment now in the technology, schools and colleges could respond to the gathering pace of technological change which requires a corresponding programme of retraining throughout employees' careers. Yet a redirection of resources to enable schools and colleges to provide all their students as well as adults returning to and retraining for work with the pre-vocational skills necessary for full computer literacy would still only provide the technical potential to create a new and unified system of education for work. A new curriculum which *facilitates* instead of *prevents* transfer between its different levels is also required. Simply, education can no longer be about selection for employment. In a modernizing economy education and training must raise the skills of all workers from the bottom up, much as literacy campaigns have aimed to do in the Third World. Education and training together will then integrate rather than separate manual and mental labour.

The resources are available for the investment required if education and training are to play their part in a programme of economic modernization and social reconstruction. As even the last Labour Chancellor Denis Healey has said, 'For Britain the first priority must be a massive switch from defence spending to economic reconstruction. Otherwise we cannot hope to repair the damage done in recent years to our economic infrastructure - our roads and railways, our schools and universities.' Such a redirection of resources to enable a comprehensive reform of education and training to 18 can prepare the way for a culture of lifelong learning and recurrent access to higher education and adult training. This will contribute to and must be part of a programme of economic modernization. The demand for reform of education and training and for a new direction for the economy and society should be presented as part of popular campaigns of 'recurring and co-ordinated protest', which, as Ken Jones says in *Right Turn* (1989, p.167), 'forms the best context for the presentation of alternative ideas.'

Chapter Six

What's Left in Teacher Education: Teacher Education the Radical Left and Policy Proposals for the 1990s

Dave Hill

There are three clients of the teacher education system. First, the national education service; second, teacher trainees/teacher education students themselves, and third the schools themselves - not only within England and Wales, but, post 1992, in the European Community. Institutions of teacher education - University Departments of Education, Polytechnics, Colleges/Institutes of Higher Education - are the producers, the providers, the developers of future teachers and also the beneficiaries of the system.

The Current Debate on Teacher Education
There are three current debates about teacher education:- those of teacher supply, teacher retention and the teacher education curriculum - how to train/educate new teachers.

This chapter makes policy proposals for the third of these: the teacher education curriculum. It is deliberately written in two register: the polemical/rhetorical and the academic.

This chapter will concentrate on the following issues within teacher education:
  (i)   its philosophy and 'model of the teacher';
  (ii) the balance of content between
        a) Main Subject,
        b) Professional Curriculum/Skill,
        c) Professional Critical/Theoretical,
        d) School experience.
  (iii) the overall amount of school experience;
  (iv) entry and exit criteria for IT (Initial Training) courses;
  (v)   length of courses;
  (vi) the nature and extent of the relationship between schools
        and colleges.

A number of perspectives about teacher education/training have emerged in recent years. Since the late 1980s in particular, following the legislative and publicity attempt to 'settle' schools and teachers, the 'Radical Right' critical spotlight has been harshly focused on teacher education.

Two current models of initial teacher education are commonly presented as alternatives to each other:

(1) the classroom competency/skills model,

(2) the reflective practitioner model.

But these are not the only models. There is a third, a 'Radical Left', model of the teacher which is a distinctive variant of the reflective practitioner model - distinctive in its pedagogy, in its Initial Teacher Education curriculum content and in its intention. This model, promulgated by this chapter, is

(3) the critical reflective 'transformative' practitioner model.

In practice longer courses such as 4-year full-time BEd (Bachelor of Education degree) courses tend to and claim to attempt to develop the reflective practitioner model, whereas many shorter courses such as the 1-year full-time PGCE (Post-Graduate Certificate in Education) decide to concentrate mainly on the competency skill model.

The PGCE course is only 36 to 37 weeks long. Approximately 14 weeks of this is commonly spent on teaching practice, leaving around 23 weeks, - 115 days - for college-based courses. The difficulties of attempting to develop in students 'reflection-in-action' or 'reflection-on-action' within such a short time are widely recognised. Many course tutors and course outlines do attempt to develop 'reflective practitioners', or even 'critical reflective transformative practitioners'. But how realistic is this within 115 days?

The apparent dichotomy or polarization between the competency/skills model of the teacher on the one hand, and the reflective practitioner model should be challenged. These are not, in my view, incompatible.

Five Perspectives on Teacher Education

Within the ideological debate there are a number of, by now quite well known, broad positions: The 'Radical Right' and 'Hard Centre' tend to argue for the classroom competency/skills model, the 'Soft Centre' and the 'Left in the Centre' for the reflective practitioner model, the 'Radical Left' for the critical reflective transformative practitioner model.

1. The Radical Right

'Radical Right' writers on education and on teacher education in Britain include the Hillgate Group, (Roger Scruton and Caroline Cox among others), Stuart Sexton, Anthony O'Hear, Dennis O'Keefe, Rhodes Boyson, Beverley Shaw and Sheila Lawlor, supported by numerous articles in *The Times, Daily Telegraph, Daily Mail* and *Times Educational Supplement*. Their writings include the flimsily researched Centre for Policy Studies Report attacking college-based teacher education by Sheila Lawlor which was accompanied by leading articles and editorial comment in a number of right-wing daily newspapers and weeklies such as the *Times Educational Supplement*, some controlled by Rupert Murdoch.[1]

Common interrelated themes of the Radical Right in respect of teacher education are that the present college-based system of teacher education should be scrapped (either totally or substantially); school based on-the-job skill development, such as the Licensed Teacher Scheme, should become the major type of teacher training; college-based teacher education is too much concerned with changing society and/or developing egalitarian or liberal perspectives on schooling and society; in particular, college-based teacher education promulgates a model of the multi-cultural and anti-racist teacher; college-based teacher education concentrates too little on classroom discipline skills; college-based teacher education is too progressive and child-centred; other than practical skills, teachers also need 'knowledge and love of the subject to be taught'; and there is no or little need for educational theory.

Three Centre Perspectives

Within this broadly Centrist group the three distinguishable sub-groups are the 'Hard Centre', the 'Soft Centre', and the 'Left in the Centre'.

2. The Hard Centre

This collection of individuals seek to accept some of the critique of the Radical Right. Such 'Hard -Centre' teacher educators, for example David Hargreaves and Mary Warnock, do not appear to be organised into formal groupings.[2] Among them there seems to be a consensus emerging about some of the below points. They see something wrong with the state of teacher education, and welcome the blowing away of the cobwebs, the opening up of these debates. They accept a combination of:

1.   easier academic entry qualifications onto Initial Training (IT) courses if it is tied to maturity and previous experience;

2.   shortened courses on the lines of the shortage subject shortened BEd 2-year courses;

3.   other models of shortage courses (of which there are few examples in England);

4.   a reduction in (effectively an attack on) reflective theory on macro- issues, radical theory and practice relating to critical theory and egalitarianism, together with an increase in time on classroom competencies and skills;

5.   virtual totally school-based siting of Initial Teacher Education (ITE) (as in the Licensed Teacher Scheme)

6.   substantially school-based siting of ITE (as in the Articled Teacher Scheme). This last view is particularly associated with David Hargreaves in a series of attacks on the BEd degree in The Times Educational Supplement.

7.   school-based siting (of the 'substantial' rather than 'total' model) either in specially selected teaching schools, (which might include City Technology Colleges), or involving a much wider use of schools, even rotating the experience to involve most or all schools.

These may well be supported not just by atavistic Radical Righters but also by some levels of college managements flexing their newly strengthened autonomous managerial muscles, delighting in shaking up existing practice and staffs. This could be seen as 'ex-lefts' engaging in managerialist power plays.

Other college teacher educators appear to act from expediency either habitually, bending to every authoritative wind that blows, or selectively, partly on the grounds of avoiding retribution, cuts in funding or cuts in student numbers. This sub-group of the Centre is not, as far as I am aware, an identifiable organized grouping nor do they all accept all seven of the proposals. In any case some of these proposals are alternatives to each other. But they seem to accept, emphasise or demand: more school-basing, more skills/competency training, less critical theory and egalitarianism, shorter courses, and easier access into teacher education and teaching.

3. The Soft Centre

This group argues that 'everything in the garden is rosy', Nirvana would exist if there were more resourcing and people would 'let us get on with the job'. This is a not untypical 'producer' view, and is the view of a number of teacher education institutions and college/university department of education lecturers. Sometimes it is borne out of genuine ideological support for those 'Plowdenite', 'comprehensivist', and sometimes, 'equal opportunities' policies in schooling and education and not simply out of the innate comfort or conservatism of not wanting to change.

4. The Left in the Centre

This group comprises individuals and networks whose ideological orientations are left of centre, sometimes a little, sometimes a lot.

Groups and initiatives have been set up by BERA (the British Education Research Association), by UCET (the Universities Council for the Education of Teachers), by 'The Future of Teacher Training' (sic) Writing Group, co-ordinated by Jean Ruddock and David Bridges, and by the 'Imaginative Projects: Arguments for a New Teacher Education' group whose publication of that name is published in January 1991.[3]

The intentions and the group writings of these various groups, however left their personal politics might be, differ little from those of the 'Soft Centre'. In some cases this derives from the politics of the lowest common denominator in opposing Radical Right attacks on teacher education. In other cases it may derive from other aspects of 'reformism' - such as moderating views in the hope of gathering wider support, wider alliances. While such initiatives are welcome for those reasons implicit in political 'reformism' or 'revisionism', they do fail to go much beyond a defence of and rationale for the *status quo* - they neglect overt and explicit issues of social justice and equality. While individually and collectively many adherents and activists in such networks are highly committed to such issues informing Initial Teacher Education, such concerns are not made explicit in their group activities, or if they are, instead of being neon-lit, they are, in places illuminated by a flickering candle.

An example of 'Left in the Centre' writing is the booklet written by Ian Hextall, Martin Lawn, Ian Menter, Susan Sidgwick, and Stephen Walker, *Imaginative Projects: Arguments for a New Teacher Education.*

In it the writers incisively analyse the Radical Right's attack on teacher education, and current developments in ITE, defining and rationalizing reflective teacher education very clearly. It is a valuable document in these respects. But it offers a limited critique and programme. In thirty-five pages it avoids explicit development of a critical arena of reflection - socio-political reflection. In the whole booklet there is one sentence on 'critical reflection on practice' and one of their five 'principles' (assumptions about the nature and purpose of education forming the basis of teacher education) is 'critical-theoretical'.

That principle is that they 'see education as a process of empowering people with the understanding and competences which increases effective participation in our society, and enables people to define and realise their identity, think critically about the world, and to change it'.

While this may well be a principle informing the writers' individual practice and perspectives it is difficult to see how it has informed their booklet in any explicit way.

While the booklet has considerable value, it could have been written by the Soft Centre.

It is too early to pass similar comments about 'The Future of Teacher Training Writing Group' convened by Jean Ruddock and David Bridges.

The highly commendable aims of that group are as follows:

1. to defend/advance a view of: teachers as intelligent, thinking practitioners; teaching as a form of practice which has constantly to be informed by sensitivity to and intelligent reflection upon what is happening in the classroom and teaching training as an activity which has to support and develop that sensitivity, intelligence and reflectiveness in practice.

2. to defend/advance the distinctive contribution which institutions of higher education have to make to the development of practice thus conceived (at the same time as valuing the

distinctive contribution that in school practitioners can make to that training in partnership with HE).

3.   to challenge and correct some of the mythology about current teacher training propagated by the 'raving right'; that current training is entirely disassociated from practical experience in schools (they seem to have no idea of the amount of time that students spend in school-based work with or without tutors); that practising teachers play no significant part in the selection, training or assessment of student teachers (they of course play a very active part in most institutions; that the curriculum of teacher training is largely determined by the ideological whims of teacher educators (they don't seem to have heard of CATE or the Secretary of State's requirements).

4.   to disentangle some of the muddle about the relationship (or otherwise) between:

  i.   the character and quality of initial training;
  ii. the recruitment and retention of teachers;
  iii. the mismatch between initial training qualifications and the posts held by large numbers of teachers.

5.   to demonstrate our own capacity to think and work creatively:

  i.   to improve the quality of initial training and develop constructive approaches to the continuing professional development of teachers;
  ii. to extend access to initial training programmes and contribute through effective programmes of professional development to the retention and career mobility of teachers;
  iii. to provide appropriate career change and retraining support for teachers;
  iv. to work in effective partnership with practising teachers.

A number of the ten Polytechnic and University signatories to that manifesto can be regarded as Left of Centre in varying degrees.

However, like the Hextall/Lawn 'Imaginative Projects' group, their collaborative intentions are, in one sense, minimalist. No doubt their intention is to maximize the breadth and depth of their embrace and impact - honourable intentions - but they are not, as a group, overtly about the development of critical reflective transformative intellectuals.

In making this criticism I am well aware that many of those involved, such as, to take one example, Donald McIntyre, have written forcefully about the need for student teacher to develop 'a critical understanding of the curriculum and pedagogy of their subject(s)' and an appreciation of the potentialities and the problems of achieving social justice in their own teaching.[18]

I am also aware that the group/network has hardly yet begun to function. But, as it stands, its five intentions, while laudable, are not Radical and are not identifiably Left. Perhaps its effects might be.

5. The Radical Left

The fifth ideological perspective is that of the Radical Left, of which the non-sectarian democratic Socialist Hillcole Group is representative.

We hold a belief in a 'bottom-up' grassroots model of Socialism rather than a monolithic 'top-down' model. The political backgrounds of the members of this Group vary in addition to holding a social class perspective, they are, as a group, strongly influenced by the anti-racist, anti-sexist, feminist, and/or anti-homophobic grassroots activism of the Left in the 1980s. Some of us have been influenced by Gramsci and resistance theorists, and by USA critical theorists and teacher educators such as Henry Giroux, Peter McLaren, Mike Apple and Ken Zeichner. Others by British and West European left models from Sweden, France, West Germany and Portugal.

This chapter is clearly written from a Radical Left perspective. It suggests that teacher education must encourage and facilitate the development of teachers who display civic courage in pursuing social justice and equal opportunities in the classroom, school and society.

The critique and proposals in this chapter differ from those of the Centre and the Radical Right. The chapter rejects total school-siting/ basing of ITE and it also rejects overwhelming school-based ITE. It rejects assaults on theory, critical reflection, social justice and egalitarianism. This chapter thus seeks to develop a policy for teacher education which could be discussed and implemented by a Labour Government. The chapter does however accept reform in ITE. But the rationale and suggested implementation of, for example, increased use of school focussing, or a national curriculum for ITE, differ from those of the Radical Right and the Centre positions. They are drawn from different ideological perspectives and have different intentions.

What Initial Teacher Education needs: A Left Ideological Perspective
Initial Teacher Education should be based on:
i. resistance to totally or overwhelmingly school-based teacher education i.e. retaining a substantial college-based role;
ii. the development of macro- and micro-theory regarding teaching and learning, in which the socio-political and economic contexts of schooling and education are made explicit;
iii the development of effective classroom skilled teachers able to interrelate and critique theory and practice - their own and that of others;
iv the development of teachers as critical 'transformative intellectuals' and democratic participative professionals and citizens.
The four points above reflect a particular view of the general and imprecise concept of 'the reflective practitioner'. This term, like the terms 'democratic' and 'community involvement', has been open to a variety of interpretations in the USA and Britain.

For example Rosaen, Roth and Lanier in their 1990 AERA paper, 'Becoming a Reflective Teacher of Subject Matter' neatly summarize Liston and Zeichman's levels, or distinct arenas of analysis and appraisal for reflective activity, that are described in the literature on reflection.

On one level, they argue, prospective teachers should reflect about the pedagogical and curricular means used to attain educational aims. Secondly they should examine and appraise the underlying assumptions and consequences of pedagogical action. Thirdly they should analyse the moral implications of pedagogical actions and the structure of schooling. One way teacher educators differ is in their view of which of these 'arenas' is an appropriate starting point for reflection in the learning-to-teach process. Another way teacher educators differ is the extent to which they consider the third arena, the moral/socio-political arena, should be included in the teacher education curriculum.

1. Reflecting on curriculum and pedagogy. Some programmes focus very specifically on one arena of reflection: helping prospective teachers to examine critically concepts related to pedagogy and curriculum as

part of their professional coursework. The assumption is that by fostering critical appraisal of course concepts through reflective activity, prospective teachers will better understand the concepts they will later need in their teaching.

2. Reflecting on theory and practice. Still others incorporate two areas of reflection in the learning-to-teach process by having students examine:

(a) curriculum and pedagogy, and

(b) the consequences of pedagogical action. An attempt is made to provide a bridge between learning of theory through professional coursework and the realities of classroom life through various types of field experiences. Reflection about the consequences of pedagogical action is often facilitated by using particular strategies such as having students conduct action research, ethnographic studies and case studies accompanied by discussions, journal writing and written cases. Thus, the starting point for learning to be a reflective teacher is learning to analyse carefully pedagogical and curriculum issues, using programme and course concepts as conceptual tools for analysis which then guide one's classroom teaching.

3. Reflecting on issues of schooling and society. Some teacher education programmes are structured to facilitate reflection in a third arena, having prospective teachers consider the moral implications of pedagogical actions and the structure of schooling as a major reflective activity. Future teachers are encouraged to confront the moral dilemmas of instruction and conditions of schooling in a deliberate fashion. They are taught to examine ways in which the structure of schooling influences classroom learning (e.g. tracking, ability grouping, curriculum selection practices).

In her paper to the 1990 AERA Annual Meeting, 'Reflection : Out on a Limb : An Intrapersonal Process and the Development of Voice', Christine Canning describes the process of reflection resulting from the redesign of the student teaching curriculum at the University of Northern Iowa in consultation with Ken Zeichner, probably the USA's most prolific radical writer on teacher education.

Although the paper refers primarily to 'arenas' of reflection 1 and 2, it is a useful addition, in its methodology, to the various examples of attempts at arena 3, i.e. those reflecting on issues of schooling and society.

This position emerges also in a number of critical Initial Teacher Education courses which are briefly set out in a number of recent books and articles. Examples are Clay, Cole and Hill's (1990), 'Black Under-Achievement in Initial Teacher Education'; 'The Citizen as 'individual' and nationalist or 'social' and internationalist? What is the role of education?' by Cole, Clay and Hill, in Mike Cole's *Education for Equality* (1990), and in Troyna and Sikes 'Putting the Why back into teacher education' in *Forum*, Autumn 1989, which describes the BA and QTS (Qualified Teacher Status) at Warwick University based on biographical life histories in the conviction that personal experiences and understanding provide an ideal basis from which to begin to explore why we, and others, hold particular beliefs and values and why we, and they, do things in certain ways. Two other courses are set out in Dave Hill's *Charge of the Right Brigade* - the mandatory third year sixty hour BEd course at West Sussex Institute of Higher Education 'Schools and Society' (1988-89), and the optional 20 hour Year One and Two BEd courses 'Contexts for Learning' at (1987-89) Brighton Polytechnic. The PGCE course at Sheffield University attempts an innovative approach to the formation of the reflective, critical, teacher and is described in *Forum*, Spring 1989.

Such courses are clear attempts at combatting current anti-theoretical and anti-critical attacks on British teacher education. In Troyna and Sikes (1990) words. 'Training students to be mere functionaries in our schools rather than educating them to assume a more creative and, dare we say it, critical role is precisely the name of the game at the moment. But should we abandon pre-service education courses entirely and hand the reins over entirely to practising teachers? We think not.'

They add, 'Research evidence suggests that many teachers continue, consciously or otherwise, to make important decisions about the organization, orientation and delivery of the formal and informal curricula on grounds which are racist, sexist and discriminatory in a range of significant ways. Should we therefore succumb to a system of teacher education/training in which these practices could well be reproduced systematically? Or should we, instead, develop pre-service courses geared towards the development of a teaching force which reflects in a critical manner on taken-for-granted assumptions, which can articulate reasons for contesting some of the conventional wisdoms about pupils, their interests and abilities, and which, ultimately, might influence future cohorts? In short, shouldn't we be encouraging students to be intellectual about being practical?'

The Current Culture Clash
The current culture clash is between what might still be called, despite Mrs Thatcher's resignation as British Prime Minister, the Thatcherite culture of privatized service and private interest culture on the one hand, against a Socialist culture of public service and public interest.

The former consensual liberal democratic culture of the 1960s and 1970s is left looking bewildered, seeking to de-ideologize education, to retreat from the culture wars and to camp out on the lowlands of pragmatism and competency training. It has retreated from egalitarianism on grounds of expediency and/or faint-heartedness. However, a number of teacher educators have put their heads above the parapet in publications or the media. These include Ted Wragg, Tim Brighouse, Maurice Craft, Diane Montgomery, Peter Newsam, Jean Rudduck, Anthony Adams, and Witold Tulasiewicz, and Bill Taylor, the Chair of CATE. Another exception was the round robin letter signed by many University teacher educators in a scathing and effective attack on two 1990 Radical Right publications, by Sheila Lawlor and Dennis O'Keefe, and various papers at the 1990 UCET Conference. Other exceptions are the two 'Left of Centre' groups discussed above. And a number of chapters in Booth, Furlong, and Wilkin's 1990 book, *Partnership in Initial Teacher Training* criticize current developments in teacher education ideologically, for example the chapters by Margaret Wilkin, by Crozier, Mentor and Pollard, and by Ted Wragg. So too does Robert Cowens' chapter in Norman Graves' 1990 collection, *Initial Teacher Education: Policies and Progress*.

Relationships between Schools and ITE Institutions.

Recent Developments
What should be the relationship between schools and institutions of critically teacher education?

The relationships between institutions for training and schools have historically tended to involve a cycle of blame, i.e. schools blaming colleges for teachers being unprepared for the real world of the classroom, and colleges, saying that students with up-to-date training meet old guard resistance in the staffroom. However alliances have historically and contemporaneously been built over issues of resourcing (The Education Alliance) and have combined in rejection of both the Licensed Teachers Scheme and testing and opting out aspects of the Education 'Reform' Act. Many groups have united to defend the dominant child-centred liberal democratic ethos of the post - Plowden era and also some of the more radical equal opportunities developments of the 1970s and the 1980s, in particular anti-sexism and anti-racism. This is particularly true of the National Union of Teachers.

The 'taken for granted' relationship between schools and institutions of teacher education typical of the 1970s and 1980s has been split asunder by:

The imposition of the National Curriculum onto the schools with accompanying statutory testing in the years 1988-1990 and its implications for Initial Teaching Education.

The introduction and evaluation of teacher education courses with more school based involvement, supported by CATE (though in a fairly modest way), trumpeted by radical right-wing think tanks and media, and adopted as a model by growing numbers of ITE academics from Right to Left.

Heads taking over a training role in their own institutions, and heads and senior teachers making a bigger contribution to college courses and in-service training.

School staff and LEA staff being more involved in the planning and evaluation of courses as recommended by the 1989 CATE criteria.

The need for college tutors to have more 'recent, relevant and substantial' teaching experience in schools. The need for shorter courses, and courses with different access and exit levels because of teacher recruitment and retention problems.

In short, alongside the current Radical Right attacks on schooling standards and on teachers there has been a series of developments seeking to render ITE less isolated from schools and to increase school teacher involvement in ITE and ITE lecturing staff involvement in schools.

This suggests a new combined role for schools and colleges, with the crossing of professional boundaries, and a willingness to examine strengths and weaknesses to the mutual benefit of both institution and the students.

What do schools want?

There are many examples in various forms of schools' responses to the products of ITE.

In a major survey of 297 probationer teachers Her Majesty's Inspectors' (HMI) document used a tripartite methodology. The HMI observed how the new teachers teach, they interviewed students for their views on how well they felt they had been prepared by the teacher training/ education, and thirdly they interviewed school teachers concerned with helping and advising probationers.

The HMI investigation published in 1988, *The New Teacher in School* highlighted areas in which 297 newly qualified teachers felt inadequately prepared by their ITE courses. Although it was carried out on students whose courses were unaffected by the CATE 1984 criteria it did itemize, in valuable detail, a number of competencies and probationer teachers' evaluations of those competencies and areas of awareness.

In a smaller scale, unpublished study of forty teachers, headteachers and advisory teachers, Waddup and Hill looked at some of the needs voiced by these 'clients'. The study identified headteachers, teachers, and advisory teachers as clients of the education system.[4]

Sample teachers' perspectives from the Waddup and Hill survey are included in the following quotes. These are representative quotes, which are not only voiced and felt needs but are understandable and admissible - needs which should be met by institutions of teacher education:

"we need teachers who are going to stay more than one year and not want to go travelling at the end of the probationary year";

"we need teachers and students who are up to date with the changes and the National Curriculum, as our staff are already trained and we don't want to keep back-tracking" "we need infant staff who know the three core subjects really well, this is more important than having a specialist subject"

"we need the current debate on reading standards, to be taken seriously, with trainees being given a through grounding in all the skill areas as well as the theory"

"we need more teachers with another language at junior level"

"we need teachers able to problem-solve well, and to relate theory to daily practice"

"we need assessment taught alongside all the curriculum subjects and not as a separate item"

"we need students to have an understanding of comparative systems of education"

"we need teachers to have a good knowledge of special needs because of integration"

"we need students to work alongside a teacher or tutor in a proper team teaching situation, planning and evaluating together individual lessons and activities"

"we believe tutors and senior teachers must have a better respect for each other and learn to work together as a team"

"we need teachers who understand how children's race, gender, and social background affect their learning and also affects how they are treated by teachers."

"It is not helpful to have teachers who have become very passive and too dependent on the institution, they have difficulty in adjusting to staffroom and to school life"

"Counselling basics and work with adults is a vital part of training, also the teacher as manager of non-teaching staff"

Half of these most common responses relate to the debate with ITE about the content of ITE courses. Approximately half also relate to the nature and extent of the relationship between schools and colleges. And, importantly, around a half (there is some overlap) of the responses also relate to the debate concerning the philosophy and model of the teacher.

It appears from this study that schools want teachers not merely to have appropriate skills, knowledge and attitudes, but to be reflective practitioners and *active critical* reflective practitioners.

School Basing, School Focusing and ITE

A number of USA studies in 1990 highlighted considerable deficiencies in school-based teacher education. These included unsatisfactory provision and mentoring of student teachers in terms of their (i) observation of teaching, (ii) pre-teaching discussions, (iii) post-teaching critique and (iv) student teacher contact with and support from the classroom teacher mentor, the school support team, the local authority 'providers', (and, where they are involved, college teacher educators). Will Britain's Articled and Licensed teachers and even college-based teacher trainees in the nineties suffer similar deficiencies?

A major implication of the United States' Wale and Irons' (1990) study, for example, is that 'mentor training needs to be expanded so that supervision becomes more than "adequate" and that it includes, in addition to clinical supervision, developing communication and conferencing skills.' Recent United States research has many lessons for the current British systems of initial teacher training - in particular for the two new school based innovations in England and Wales (the one-year Licensed Teacher scheme which started in 1989 and the two-year Articled Teacher scheme which started its mentor training in Summer 1990 and its student teaching/teacher education course in September 1990). It also has implications for partially school-based schemes such as the WSIHE Crawley BEd degree, the Sussex University PGCE, the Oxford Polytechnic PGCE, the now defunct school based East Anglia PGCE, and a variety of schemes yet to be developed.

The reflection does arise that, however wonderful, well-paid, well trained, well-resourced, beautifully collaborative, diligent and committed mentors are, predominantly or totally school-based schemes of initial teacher education are defective. They are defective and inadequate because of their very nature. Such schemes are likely to lack:

1.   theoretical inputs;
2.   non-school based student collaborative reflective discussions.

Without adequate time for both of these, student teachers, articles, and licensed teachers may become in effect second class teachers, being treated as 'beginner teachers' rather than 'learner teachers'.

Reflectiveness and, more importantly, critical reflectiveness is likely to be diminished, demeaned, and disregarded. That is, of course, subject to teacher, mentor, new teacher, teacher union, and teacher educator resistance. If such critical reflectiveness is suppressed, that will be another triumph for the ideology of Thatcherism/Reaganism.

Most vitally, such de-theorizing school-based narrow skill competency based developments in Initial Teacher Education are subject to the policy reviews and initiatives of an incoming Labour Government. How much of current Conservative teacher education policy will the Labour Party accept and maintain? And what will it charge? What opportunities for equality and quality will it seize and develop?

Developments in Labour Party policy.

Ten policy proposals for teacher education
The Labour Party has recently produced two policy documents on education - *'Children First'* in 1989 and *'Aiming High - Raising standards in Britain's schools'* in December 1990.

'Children First' contains a number of proposals for teacher education (which it unfortunately calls 'teacher training').

The second, briefer, document includes two paragraphs specifically on what it, again calls 'teacher training':

> Labour will introduce a national core curriculum for teacher training. Training institutions will not only certify that teachers are competent to teach, but will also provide a profile of students' strengths and weaknesses as a foundation for support and supervision during their first years in the profession.
>
> We will set up teacher training schools. At present most of the initial, on-the-job training takes place in those schools with the largest number of vacancies and highest turnover - precisely the schools where pressures on the rest of the teaching staff make them likely to be under the greatest stress.

This section will set out a number of policy proposals which Labour should implement. The first six of these proposals are related to and a commentary on a critical expansion of the 1989 Labour proposals.

Continuing Teacher Education beyond Initial Qualification
The suggestion that the system of Initial Teacher Training must be recast, and must cover not only the period of college-based training, but the first five years of service, is necessary though I am not convinced about the necessity for five year period. The concern with the new teachers' 'abrupt induction' into full-time teaching, with little of a settling-in or induction period for novice teachers, is of considerable importance. It is important however not to relegate initial teacher education to deal with practical skills and leave post-qualification, or in-service training to develop theory, as suggested in general by the Radical Right. Nor must the 'critical/social/ideological' arena of reflection be excluded from college-based critical Teacher Education.

There are a number of reasons for opposing such a development. It would, in effect, separate practice from theory, training in classroom skills from educating student teachers to reflect on their own and others actions in schools.

One reason for opposing the skills first, theory and reflection afterwards approach is that for many teachers 'afterwards' in the form of post-qualification In-Service education never arrives.

There is a major danger that Labour will succumb to the proposal for skills based initial teacher education followed by 'reflective' in-service education.

Many teachers escape from in-service education. Reflective or critical reflective theory based courses might have only a minority recruitment among teachers. Furthermore an assumption that INSET (In-Service education for teachers) is reflective, is not necessarily the case. Much INSET is skills based and essentially non-reflective i.e., it is 'how to', rather than 'why to or why not to'.

Another reason is that teachers should be reflective and critically reflective from Day One of their teaching, and indeed on their teaching practices and school experience. Reflection and reflecting should inform the whole of their development as teachers and as intellectuals, with theory and practice critically informing each other.

A third reason is that induction into reflection and critical reflection is better achieved as a process, a long-term process during initial teacher education, advanced by discussion as 'learner teachers' rather than 'beginner teachers' caught up in daily, grinding, frenetic day-to-day fully timetabled teaching.

In the light of the immense and unique responsibilities placed upon newly qualified teachers, and the virtual collapse of induction and probationer programmes, Labour's proposal for say 12 weeks off-school training, based upon their training institution, within their first five years is welcome. Whether 12 weeks is enough, and whether it is feasible to base this upon training institutions needs discussing. It would certainly facilitate college evaluation of their own BEd and PGCE courses. But it is probably better achieved as part of a funded probationer and new teacher in-service support programme extending the best of current practice.

Recommendation

There should be funded induction programmes for all new teachers taking place in off school-site courses, and this funded induction should be part of an entitlement in-service professional development programme over the first five years of school-teaching service.

Core Curriculum for Initial Teacher Education

Much of this section of this chapter concerns what new teachers should know about, what skills they should possess, and what dispositions they should exhibit. While there is value in 'letting a hundred flowers bloom', in some heterogeneity between different courses of initial teacher education, in school staffs having a complementarity of areas of knowledge, there is legitimate concern that some courses are not sufficiently critically reflective, not sufficiently school focussed with too little time in schools, and do not develop classroom skills sufficiently. Everything in the garden is not rosy, although the blooms are brighter following implementation of the CATE 1984 criteria. However there is a wide difference between the fertilizing suggested here and the indiscriminate spraying of Radical Right 'weedkiller' or 'college and theory killer' which would stunt the whole garden.

Recommendation

Labour's discussion proposal for a national core curriculum for 'teacher training' should be considered in the light of what it should contain and it should be informed by the policy proposals in this chapter, by the voices of teachers, and by distinctive critical reflective content and pedagogy. It should contain school experience, subject studies, professional studies (teaching skills, management skills, how to teach subjects) and also wider critical reflective concerns of what schooling and education are for, what they should be like, and whose interests they do or should serve.

Profiling of teacher education students
The question of a profile of student's strengths and weaknesses might become acceptable but, only after looking at what sort of profile is proposed.

The HMI 'New Teacher in School' checklist is somewhat restricted and technicist in nature as an embryonic profile, and various USA profiles are even more technicist. But the use of a profile during initial teacher education and also to be continued during a funded induction period of some years, makes sense. This should be seen as part of a mutually agreed staff development programme. Such profiles are being developed on a number of ITE courses. There are a number of examples of profiling in existence which have tried to take on board criticisms of the behaviourist 'tick in the box' observable performance method of profiling.

Recommendation
Profiling of student teacher achievement should be developed, but should refer not only to skills, knowledge and attitudes, but also to student teacher reflectiveness. This should include not just the ability to analyse and evaluate within a classroom and school context, but also within a societal context. And in addition to the 'ability' to analyse and evaluate, student teacher records of achievement should include the willingness to do so.

More School Teaching Practice within the Context of a College-Based Course
The present amount of time spent in schools on most BEd and PGCE courses is ludicrously brief, as set out in section one of this chapter. Commonly the equivalent of 14 or so weeks out of a course time of 36 or 37 weeks on PGCE courses is spent in schools. And on BEd courses commonly around 20 weeks or equivalent is spent in school out of a 132 week course. The problem is, if more teaching practice gets added to

ITE courses, what gets taken out? The next proposal seeks to suggest an answer to this problem.

There is nothing intrinsically wrong with the Labour Party proposal to set up BEd three year and one term with say, the final year including a 40 week teaching practice. However, bearing in mind the need for time and space for student group reflection, pain and laughter, such teaching practice should include regular weekly time off for such purposes. For example, students could meet every Friday afternoon during teaching practice for mutually supportive and evaluative group small group discussion.

There are a variety of models for increasing block and serial school experience. Such models as those of Oxford University, Sussex University and the University of East Anglia have received a degree of publicity and there are other courses which are innovative in this respect. Such courses are the early years BEd at Brighton Polytechnic, the WSIHE Crawley BEd and ITE courses at Thames Polytechnic.

Recommendation

Whatever models of teaching practice/school experience are used, ITE courses should become substantially more school-focused, with students spending more time in schools.

Mentoring and Triangularity of Co-operation between Schools, Colleges and Students

All courses of ITE should become more school based. One model here might be the Crawley BEd in which a percentage (.25 to .5) of most education/professional courses is school based. Students are to spend around 100 days in school in addition to their block teaching practices of 18 weeks. Some of these block practices could also be lengthened.

There would be some benefit in adopting the Labour Party suggestion that new teachers should be supervised in school by designated teacher tutors, who would be rewarded for this responsibility. This has certainly been a source of angst and concern during various Summer 1990 Articled Teacher Mentor Training programmes in England which I have investigated. Not only must the school mentors be rewarded (one mentor's comment 'I am doing this for the money' possibly reflects one major mentor consideration), but teacher educator professional tutors must also have their (partly vacation-time) commitment rewarded too.

Otherwise some will not attend the mentor training sessions, and bang goes the triangularity of the college-school-student enterprise.

Supervision of students needs to be a triangular enterprise involving a partnership between college/university tutors, teachers and students. Triangularity is a well-established and fundamental feature of IT-INSET (Initial Training - In-Service Education for Teachers) components of many BEd and PGCE courses involving the working together in a classroom of a classteacher, a college tutor, and a group of around six or seven students on a regular basis over a period of time. Planning, observation and evaluation are carried out jointly in post-session teams. IT-INSET is one of the best extant examples of triangularity in British teacher education.

Teacher 'mentors' or 'teacher-co-operators', in both pre-service and post-qualification modes, need reward and time and training to enable 'high-intensity' mentoring to take place. In a number of ITE courses 'teacher co-operators' are being offered a combination of cash and certification.

In order for schools to play a far more active role in the management, development, teaching, and mentoring of student teachers, school mentors need to be compensated in terms of certification, honoraria or supply cover time off school and by mentor training, and support groups.

The rationale for this can be found in the widespread inadequacies reported in the USA mentor teacher schemes, and reactions by schools to a variety of British mentor based or 'teacher-co-operator' based developments.

Recommendation

School mentors should be paid, trained and certificated.

Use of Client Schools as 'Teacher Education/Professional Development Schools'

The Labour proposal that 'teacher training schools' would be established has some advantages. Certainly a number of courses build a very close relationship with a small number of schools rather than a loose relationship with a large number of schools, involving headteachers and whole or substantial parts of school staffs in Initial Teacher Training. Various papers discuss the need for closer co-operation and for support from principals/heads. On a number of courses Headteachers and 'teacher co-operators' are involved in course development, prior to, as well as after validation, course management, interviewing of students, and it is desirable for 'teacher co-operators' to have regular meetings as a team with the appropriate team of tutors. Indeed many of these developments stem from the 1989 requirements of CATE, the Committee for Accreditation of Teacher Education.

Labour's suggestion of rotating the benefits of teacher training schools seems sensible too, one of the benefits being the in-service development that should and can go with the professional role of co-operating in the development of entrants to the profession.

Recommendation
Schools should be designated Teacher Education Schools/Professional Development Schools both for the in-service development of those schools and for the effective preparation and education of student teachers. Such schools should be designated on a rotating basis.

Recommendation
There should also be a continuous negotiated debate and partnership between schools and institutions of ITE, with for example, the CATE criteria of 1989 being actually implemented in practice and not just in claims.

Teacher Assistants, Entry and Exit Levels for ITE Courses
The call by the Labour Party (1989) for 'a proper structure for teacher assistants' and for 'the qualifications and experience of teachers' assistants to be fairly reflected as credits towards a teacher qualification' are both welcome. The quality, experience and insights gained by many of the mature entrants to BEd courses that I have interviewed (and taught) in the last few years are staggering. The Labour policy document suggests that 'while we are firmly of the opinion that teaching should be an all-graduate profession and that there should be one exit level from training, there should be different entry levels.'

This has to be welcomed, but cautiously. The Licensed Teacher scheme and the Radical Right have advanced similar arguments. Exit levels and exit competency profiles need to be more than merely technicist. Moreover, some pre-course school experience/field experience may have an admirable quantitative dimension but not necessarily as admirable a qualitative dimension. And so it is necessary for Labour 'to discuss with' (various bodies including) 'the training institutions, how this greater flexibility might be achieved.' This could involve giving credit for evaluated pre-course field or allied field experience, and possibly involving a substantial - I would suggest no more than four days a week - teaching experience for some terms in some years, particularly in the final year of the BEd degree. But in the role of 'learner teachers' rather than 'beginner teachers.'

There should be easier entry in ITE for potential recruits with suitable APEL (Alternative Prior Experience and Learning) on the model of the Mature Entry Scheme already in operation in a number of Institutions of ITE. Examples are the Mature Entry Scheme to the WSIHE BEd and BA courses, and to undergraduate courses at some of the London Polytechnics such as the Polytechnic of North London, Thames Polytechnic, South Bank Polytechnic.

Recommendation

Teaching should remain an all-graduate profession.

Recommendation

Access to Teacher Education should be widened by a more substantial adoption by ITE institutions of APEL (Assessment of Prior Experience and Learning) procedures, and such experience as Teacher Assistants should be valued and positively assessed.

Recommendation

There should be sub-degree level certification for Teacher Assistants.

Shortened Courses

Short two-year BEd courses should be established for all subjects of the Primary Curriculum and Secondary Curriculum but strictly related to the point made about continuing teacher education beyond initial qualification above. This is not meant to imply an abandonment of four year degrees, nor to open the door (*à la* Licensed Teachers Scheme) to clapped out executives who fancy, or are pushed into, a change. It recognises instead that for some groups of professional workers trained/ educated in human relations such as sub-degree level social workers or ESL assistants, and suitably certificated teacher assistants, there needs to be a course between the existing 1-year and 4-year in length.

A number of higher education institutions already give credit exemption for previous experience. With credit accumulation degrees students with appropriate prior learning and experience can be and are given accelerated progress through degrees in some institutions, but this has not yet become a systematic practice. The proposal for a 2 year BEd is a proposal separate from the above individualised practice of individuals proceeding through four year BEds at an accelerated rate.

However this should not be a quick fix or a short cut to a sexist over-loading of Primary Schools with under-trained, under-educated women, induced or compelled to enter the labour market. Such recruits, indeed all recruits, need high quality teacher education, unless English/Welsh teachers are to be regarded as second rate in Europe after 1992, unqualified to teach for example in Germany or France.

It would be ironic if, because of developments in total or overwhelmingly school-based initial teacher education, and because of shortening of BEd courses on a wide scale, newly trained school teachers were to become the educational pariahs of Western Europe. This is a danger, that newly trained school teachers might be regarded as under-qualified to teach in Germany or France, qualified only to take jobs as teachers' assistants. In Portugal there has been deliberate government policy to switch from school-based teacher education to college-based teacher education. One of the acknowledged reasons is to raise the quality of new Portuguese, teachers to meet European Community standards.

Recommendation

There should be an expansion of shortened and part-time BEd courses, recognising the limited time within shortened courses available for a full 'over a period of time' development of a critical reflective teacher.

Recommendation

There should be post-entry requirement for in-service education for shortened course teachers, of one year of in-service development within the first five years of teaching.

Longer PGCE School-focussed/based Courses

On Articled Teacher courses there has been concern among teacher educators, school mentors, class teachers, and articlees themselves about the need for more college-based input (in particular on non-curriculum and non-management issues) for example on the social contexts of schooling. There have been calls for more opportunity for critical collaborative reflection and evaluation in a non-threatening environment. This is a form of resistance to the skills-based uncritical model of the teacher advanced by the 'Radical Right'.

On existing one year PGCE courses, such is the shortage of time in a 36 or 37 week course, that students in general do not have enough space or time to cope with the pain, laughter, and blitzkrieg effect of their school practice. They lack the necessary luxury of time both for collaborative and sympathetic recuperation and for systematic reflective collaborative evaluation over a period of time.

Recommendation

PGCE courses should become two-year courses on the model of the Articled Teacher, with students, as 'learner-teachers', being paid as on the present non-means tested bursary system for their two years. However instead of the course being 80 per cent in school and 20 per cent in college the ratio should be more like 3 days a week in schools for two years and two days a week in college ie 60 per cent/40 per cent or 65 per cent/35 per cent. This is similar, in terms of payment, to the current (West) German model of teacher education.

Critical Reflective Teachers

Teacher education must be concerned with and attempt to encourage the development of teachers as effective classroom practitioners who are, at the same time, 'critical reflective teachers' and 'transformative intellectuals'. Among the implications of these phrases are that these teachers should be capable of, and willing, to blow peoples' minds - their own, their pupils', their colleagues' - to open up choices, alternative histories, presents and futures, to develop in themselves and in others, democratic, and critical citizenship and action both in the micro- societies of the classroom, staffroom, school, and teacher union branch, and in the wider society.

These are bold, and yet not novel, intentions. They are important at this juncture of British and Western capitalist economic, political and ideological development. At the ideological level, the Thatcher-Reagan economic-market/morally-authoritarian, vituperatively anti-egalitarian attack on teacher education, has generated legislation and rhetoric which seek to bring into line, to 'thought-control', and to ideologize more effectively the schooling and teacher education parts of the state apparatus. The attempt is to de-theorize and destroy current teacher education, and to replace it with skills based, national curriculum and assessment led, uncritical teacher training.

Teachers have a duty, and should be educated into seeing their task not simply as fitting children into largely predetermined roles in the labour market, or slotting them into uncritical quiescent acceptance of immoral market barbarism. Thatcherism created and fed upon envy, consumerism, selfishness, a 'tread on your neighbour mentality', glorifying an élite while intensifying divisions in society. Children need to be able to analyse existing society, to discuss and design alternative futures for themselves and their communities.

The 'Radical Right' wishes to take teacher education out of colleges and submerge trainee teachers in the rush of classroom survival with no time to reflect on and evaluate more socially valid and concerned visions of schooling and education. And the 'Hard Centre' is willing to go along with many of their proposals. But all children should be taught to think for themselves, to evaluate, to reflect, to analyse.

If trainee teachers become apprentices, learning, like butchers, on the job - they will know their dead meat and they will know how to cut it. One dead sheep is pretty much like another. But children are alive. Teachers need more than subject knowledge and classroom skills. They need to reflect on the why and why not, the individual and group similarities and differences and needs. One child can be very different from another and so can its life chances and experience of schooling - and what it needs from its teachers.

Teacher, teacher educators and parents must resist narrow restrictive and restricted competency and skills based teacher training. And insist on and develop critical reflective teachers and society.

Recommendation

All courses should retain a substantial college based element to facilitate the induction over a period of time into professional ethos, concern, awareness, and to enable students to develop reflectively as reflective evaluative and critical practitioners.

These are ten policy recommendations for initial teacher education. In addition there is the necessity of resourcing.

Adequate funding for Teacher Education

It is absolutely ludicrous that, at a time of a major shortage of teachers, institutions of teacher education in the Polytechnics and Colleges sector are being penalized financially for recruiting above PCFC target figures in Summer 1990. This has the effect that student teachers recruited 'above target' in September 1990 are being under funded, that is to say, Polytechnics and Colleges are receiving hundreds of pounds less income per 'over target' student. This punishment is having the effect of causing a number of institutions to cut back on student teacher recruitment for 1991.

Recommendation

There should be funding for enough teachers to meet the current teacher shortage.

Conclusion

As a conclusion to this discussion teacher educators, and the Labour Education Team must not get swept along in a reactionary Victorian value tidal wave emulating Conservative policy willy-nilly.

The emancipatory, critical, and transformatory role of educators and of education and schooling must not be submerged by the twin waves of concern over teacher shortage and over 'practical skills'.

While accepting that the school-based element of current English BEd and PGCE courses should be increased, teachers, teacher educators, and political decision makers such as Jack Straw should resist current attempts to take the theory out of teacher education, take the critical thinking out of teachers minds, and take teacher education wholesale out of colleges.

Notes

1. See Sheila Lawlor *Teachers Mistaught: training in theories or education in subjects?* (London: Centre for Policy Studies). Sheila Lawlor also wrote 'Something is Wrong in the Classroom', *The Daily Telegraph*, 11 June 1990
2. David Hargreaves' views have been set out in a series of articles in the *Times Educational Supplement*. See 'Judge radicals by results', *Times Educational Supplement*, 6 October 1989; 'Out of BEd and into Practice,' *Times Educational Supplement*, 8 September 1989; 'PGCE assessment fails the test,' *Times Educational Supplement* 3 November 1989; 'Looking at a model of health,' *Times Educational Supplement*, 1 December 1989; 'Another Radical Approach to the Reform of Initial Teacher Training' Paper delivered at UCET Conference,

London, (1990). See also 'Remission as a Life Sentence : Flexibility is the key to teacher training,' *Times Higher Education Supplement* 21 September 1990.

3. The British Educational Research Association (BERA) research group on teacher education includes Jack Whitehead, David Hustler, John Elliott, Jean Rudduck, Dave Hill. The UCET group (Universities Council for the Education of Teachers) embraces a wide number of University teacher educators. The 'Future of Teacher Training Group' is open to teacher educators across the binary (University/Polytechnic and College) divide, and the 'Imaginative Projects Group' publication is in press. As well as the writers (Ian Hextall, Martin Lawn, Ian Menter, Susan Sidgwick and Steven Walker), this involved initially, though not finally, Colin Lacey, Dave Hill and Geoff Whitty. Organized resistance to current attacks on theory based and on college-based education has become evident in 1990 and 1991.

As organizations BERA and UCET do not have a specific political orientation, and are more heterogeneous politically that the other two specific issue groups mentioned here. Having said that though, the teacher education papers at the 1989 and 1990 BERA Conferences were in general highly critical of Radical Right developments in ITE, and, in general, very supportive of the reflective practitioner model. And the UCET press statement is similarly caustic about (two of) the Radical Right attacks on 'teacher training'. However, I agree with the UCET Press statements refutation of the charge that 'teacher training is socialist'.

4. This research consisted of soliciting forty teachers' opinions on 'what do schools want from new teachers fresh out of their initial teacher education courses?' The research used unprompted verbal interviews and written questionnaire questions. The fourteen statements recorded here were the most common responses.

Chapter Seven

Resources and Funding for State Education

Rehana Minhas and Gaby Weiner

Context

Over the last decade the conflict between the Conservative Central Government, under the leadership of Mrs. Thatcher, and local government has heightened, as the ideological shift to the Right has involved a remodelling of the state apparatus. The ideological conflict has been more acute between central government and Labour-controlled inner city Councils. Labour Councils have been systematically attacked by the Radical Right for their commitment to 'Welfare Socialism' and to equal opportunities. As Stephen Ball has argued,[1] the Radical Right, drawing on the political and economic theories of Friedrich Hayek, are opposed to the idea of a Welfare State. Hayek regards state provision of health, social services and education, derived from tax revenues, as unfair, inefficient and as tending to reduce incentive and innovation. Hayek is particularly critical of those government policies which attempt to redistribute wealth and resources based on ideas of social justice. The 1980s were the period when many local authorities began formulating equal opportunities policies, with a commitment to redress the existing inequalities. 'Riots or 'uprisings' nationally had forced inner-city authorities to address issues of race, class and gender inequalities. Thus it was not surprising that such Labour Authorities were accused by the Central Government, through the media of 'high spending,' which was attributed to mismanagement, political indoctrination, and for being large unresponsive bureaucracies which denied individual freedom and choice. The abolition of the Greater London Council (GLC) in April 1986 and of the ILEA in April 1990 are just two examples of the severe measures taken by the Central Government to 'resolve' opposition from local government, in spite of the support from their local constituents.

The main basis of the conflict has been the Conservative Government's commitment to a Radical Right ideology of free market philosophy. The

Radical Right ideology has been implemented through the development of a programme entailing monetarism, large-scale privatization, the dismantling of the Welfare State, and policies seeking to preserve 'traditional British culture' which is exclusive, racist, sexist and anti-working class; in short a remodelling of the local state. This remodelling has been attempted mainly through legislation designed to control the activities of local government. The cuts in public expenditure, and tighter financial controls have been secured through a succession of Local Government Acts, as have been measures to 'curtail political indoctrination'.

The 1980 Local Government (Planning and Land) Act introduced the Support Grant penalties. Further constraints took place with the introduction of rate-capping in 1985/86. This package of financial constraints has been further consolidated by the introduction of the community charge and 'capping'. Central Government controls on capital expenditure have been tightened to prevent 'asset stripping' i.e. local authorities raising revenue by the sale of property. There has been a major reduction in grant to Local Authorities from the Central Government since the 1980s and this trend is likely to continue. The impact of these major legislative changes affecting local government have, when taken together, radically altered the role of local authorities and in particular their ability to provide quality services in response to local needs. Equal opportunities policies which have involved a process of re-allocating resources to alleviate the most damaging impact of poverty, racism and sexism have become increasingly impossible to implement.

In this chapter we focus on the impact of the legislative changes on the resources and funding for education. Throughout the 1980s, the Conservative Government sought to curtail the power and influence of the democratically elected local education authorities through funding policy in *two* ostensibly contradictory ways. On the one hand, it centralized important elements of LEA expenditure by taking to itself the administration of the funding of INSET and by encouraging educational innovations such as TVEI through 'categorical' funding. On the other hand, it devolved responsibility for the bulk of the general expenditure on education to governing bodies of schools and of colleges through the Education 'Reform' Act 1988. The components of the Act, open enrolment, local management of schools/colleges combined with financial constraints on local government and changes in funding are designed to introduce into education the competition of market forces. This political perspective regards competition as a necessity for efficient management and sees the managing of educational institutions as being no different from that of commercial institutions.[2] Phillip Brown and Hugh Lauder argue strongly that 'free market reforms in education are neither in the interests of the vast majority of people despite the rhetoric of freedom and choice, nor are they in the national economic interest. They are geared to preserving the privileges and power of the minority, at a time of profound social and economic change'.[3]

Since the abolition of the ILEA, there has been a debate within the Conservative Party on the desirability or otherwise of removing education from local authority control. A substantial amount of local government expenditure is spent on providing education services. This debate surfaced at the beginning of 1991 and involved the floating of a number of ideas within Conservative ranks. It was revealed in March 1991 that the Major Government was giving serious consideration to policies which would *both* create a single tier of local government *and* transfer the responsibility for large sections of education from local authorities to Central Government. The Government clearly intended to bring the £17bn education service under direct central control to the point where local education authorities were either axed or left to wither away and die. In the event, the proposals announced by Michael Heseltine, the Secretary of State for the Environment, on 21 March 1991 did not include plans for a sudden switch of the funding of schools from local government to Whitehall, the Government, and in particular Kenneth Clarke, preferring that the pace of change should be determined by the rate at which schools opted out of local authority control.

Details of the Financing of Education

Background
Education is one of the largest consumers of public money. For example, in 1986/87, the total expenditure on education was £15.7bn, some 11.2 per cent of all public spending. In that year, 61 per cent went to schools, nearly all on salaries and services; 29 per cent was spent on Further and

Higher Education, again on salaries and services; and the rest was spent on the relatively slight costs of administration and research councils.

In real terms, spending on education remained constant until 1985/ 6 and after a dip in 1985/6, has since risen slightly. However, it has *decreased* markedly as a proportion of total government expenditure from 5.5 per cent in 1981/2 to 4.8 per cent in 1985/6.

The cost of education has generally been shared between central and local government. Much of central government's direct expenditure has been conventionally concerned with specific grants, for example, payments to universities and research councils or targeted grants for purposes such as in-service training. Local government has controlled the largest part of expenditure, 84 per cent in 1989, according to Statham, Mackinnon and Cathcart,[4] and has been responsible for employing staff, maintaining premises and buying equipment.

The Structure of Funding Policy-prior to April 1990
The 1980s were characterized by disagreements between LEAs and Central Government about what constituted 'adequate' spending on education. Not only was this disagreement concerned with the level of educational expenditure, but also with financial allocation.

The yearly funding cycle is as follows: the Government publishes a public spending White Paper which outlines expenditure on education over the next few years: representatives from central and local government then meet to set the figure for each authority's spending in the next financial year and decide the proportion of the total expenditure to be raised locally. In the mid-1970s, for example, the grant percentage rose to 66.5 per cent; by 1979 it had slipped to 61 per cent, and in 1987, it was 46.3 per cent.[5]

Previously *Grant Related Entitlement* (GRE) i.e. the proportion of overall grant going to each authority, was calculated according to a highly complex and bureaucratic procedure, according to:

a) LEAs scores on a range of factors which affect their rate of spending e.g. number of immigrants', low socio-economic groups, substandard housing, one-parent families, families in receipt of benefit and so on.

b) Penalties for 'overspending' i.e. spending above the Government's stipulated level. Once LEAs have overstepped the GRE figure by more than 10 per cent, the Government reduces the Block Grant and induces an increase in the proportion of funding from local sources (legalized in the Local Government Finance Act, 1982). This procedure robbed the ILEA of its total entitlement to Block Grant in the 1980s. The Government has also moved to restrict local funding which exceeds Government targets (Rates Act, 1984) and has given itself, for the first time, powers to set an upper limit to rate (and poll tax) increases where they are judged to be excessive.

c) The choice of fund which makes grant allocation. There are four elements of Government grant to education:

Block Grant accounting for three quarters of total Government grants to LEAs;

Domestic Rate Relief aimed at keeping the rates or poll tax down;

Specific Grants for, for example, urban aid;

Supplementary Grants for transport and in-service training.

The changes in the structure of funding policy, since April 1990.

The Aggregate External Finance (AEF) for local government services, comprises three elements: the yield from business rates, specific grants and Revenue Support Grant.

The total of AEF for 1990/1991 would be made up as follows:

	£ million
Revenue Support Grant	9,490
Inner London Education Special Grant	100
Low rateable value areas Special Grant	87
Other Specific Grants within AEF	2,995
National Non-domestic Distributable Amount (NNDR)	10,428
Total AEF	23,100bn

In order to distribute the Revenue Support Grant, the Secretary of State for the Environment requires an assessment for each authority of what it would cost to provide services locally to a common standard. The method for making these assessments, known as the Standard Spending Assessments (SSAs, see appendix to this chapter) has replaced Grant Related Expenditure Assessments. The rationale for this change is that the Grant Related Expenditure Assessments (GRE) had become over complex and difficult to explain. In place of the 63 separate assessments in the previous GRE system, there are now 13 components: 11 covering the five major services (education, social services, fire and civil defence, police and highway maintenance), another covering all other services, and one reflecting the financing costs of capital expenditure. In general, the method introduced involves fixing a unit cost of providing each service and multiplying this by the number of clients for that service.

SSAs are central to the new grant system, for they determine the community charge for a given area. It is important to note the significance of this change. All government spending decisions are based on SSA and not on what local authorities actually spend. The 'bench mark' for accountability of the community charge has been set by the Government at £278. In this new system of revenue the community charge is set by local authorities (with an eye to the penalty of being 'capped'). Central Government sets the National non-domestic rate and the revenue support grant. (Previously the Rates, domestic and non-domestic were set by local authorities). One of the immediate impacts of the community charge has been the reduction in revenue for a large number of local authorities who have a low collection rate.

General impact on local authorities
The list of cash starved authorities increases rapidly, and these are by no means confined to Labour controlled authorities. A survey of 17 Tory authorities which cut their budgets in 1991 found evidence that the National Curriculum, inspection and advisory service had already suffered in past years. The biggest cut was found in Kent, where £8.2 million was taken from education. The county is closing all its 11 careers centres with the loss of 109 jobs, and is to reduce staff in its inspectorate and advisory service from 198 to 133.

Cuts in Tory LEAS (all figures are in £Mn)
(taken from the *Times Educational Supplement* 15 March 1991)
The impact on the disadvantaged inner city councils is even greater. Up to 50 per cent of teaching vacancies in Liverpool schools may not be filled and this is in addition to a £1.8 million package of education cuts. In Lambeth 320 full time equivalent jobs will be lost in education and adult education spending will be cut by 40 per cent. In Haringey the council has to cut 1200 jobs. Education and in particular the support services, central administration, inspection and advisory services have borne the brunt of the cuts.

Local government expenditure has fallen in real terms over the past decade; in 1980 it was 8.5 per cent of Gross Domestic Product and in 1989 7.2 per cent. Rates or charges went up because the proportion of Central Government grant was reduced during the same period. We would argue that far from a policy of devolution, the Government policy has been one of eroding local democracy and centralizing control. The extent of cuts in local government are national and can no longer be explained in terms of 'irresponsible high spending local authorities'.

The impact of the 1988 Act
Until the recent changes in funding, LEA expenditure was proportionally spent as follows: 52 per cent on salaries for teaching staff; 13.2 per cent on other salaries; 10.1 per cent on premises; 7.6 per cent on awards and allowances; 5.1 per cent on school milk and meals; and 2.6 per cent on equipment, 2.2 per cent on transport, 0.7 per cent on books and 6.3 per cent for other sundry items.

However, the 1988 Education 'Reform' Act has changed this funding partnership by dramatically reducing the percentage of educational expenditure within the remit of the LEAs. Under its terms, polytechnics and larger colleges have become self-governing; all secondary schools and primary schools with more than 200 pupils have been delegated with responsibility for the financial management of their institutions, and this will soon be extended to all small schools. By 1 April 1993, 80 per cent of the delegated budget must be directly linked to the number of pupils, with up to 20 per cent based on other factors of need. The philosophy of free market forces now enters education. Pupils are seen as 'financial assets', generating income. The general impact of the 1988 Act is to limit the powers of Local Education Authorities and tightly prescribe their pattern of expenditure through formula funding. The Education Reform Act allows schools to opt out of Local Authority control by seeking Grant Maintained Status (GMS), which requires the approval of the Secretary of State for Education. As schools opt out of local authority control, the general schools budget for the authority concerned is reduced.[6]

Local Management of Schools

LMS is more than mere financial delegation to schools. It represents a major ideological change in the process and dynamics of educational management, which is having a fundamental effect on educational provision in state schools. The popular rationale for Local Management of Schools (LMS) is that decision making at local level, when underpinned by control over resources, will lead to a better service. It is highly mechanistic and problematic to assume that the existence of a scheme of local management can in itself improve the quality of teaching and learning at a time of reduced public expenditure. LMS has thus diverted funds so that the bulk of financial management has been delegated to schools and LEAs are responsible for only a small percentage of educational expenditure. Even this small amount of expenditure is tightly controlled: the Secretary of State must approve all local authority funding formulae. Already unfair decisions have been made: recently 'homelessness' was accepted in the calculations of Westminster, but rejected for Newham. Also carefully developed LEA procedures for pupil admissions and staff appointments are likely to suffer as school Governors and Headteachers make decisions on the basis of school interest and/or financial considerations.

The Association of Educational Psychologists has reported a big increase in demand for psychological services, prompted by changes to local government and educational finance, which have increased the number of applications for statements for children with special needs. The number of referrals increased by between 40 and 60 per cent in most areas. Due to formula funding LEAs have also found themselves unable to give the same level of additional help to those schools with great educational problems.

Formula induced under-funding

Early evidence suggests that many schools are suffering due to formula induced under-funding. Governing bodies are having to choose in experienced staff, as they cost less. Teachers salaries under the formula are worked out on an average and do not account for the real wages i.e. the range within the salary spine. The most vulnerable are inner city schools, with a majority working class and black and ethnic minority intake. Small schools in rural areas have also been badly hit.

Open enrolment

Open enrolment is seen as essential in creating competition between schools. The Tory logic is that 'good' schools will survive and the bad ones will ' sink'. This notion is very simplistic and does not take into account the geographical differences within the authority and also, patterns of settlement which have been determined historically by race and class inequalities. What it does is to give affluent parents a choice to buy education for their children away from the state system. In practice not all parents have a choice of schools for their children.

Governing bodies

Financial viability is an added variable to the funding scenario. LMS assumes that all schools (that is, Governors and Headteachers) will be able to handle their finances. What will happen if a school goes bankrupt or is unable to manage its finances? Will the LEA or DES assume responsibility or might the school close? How might this affect the quality or inequality of educational provision for its pupils?

Local Management of Colleges (LMC)

This is a parallel development to LMS, but for Further and Higher Education. Its main provision is to grant self-governing status to colleges and polytechnics. This again has implications for the quality or inequality of educational provision: whether, for example, carefully established LEA guidelines on good practice and procedures underpinning race and gender policies will be allowed to continue.

Financial inducements for Grant Maintained Schools

Grant Maintained Schools receive a lump sum averaging £25,000 to cushion their switch to GM status. They have had their budgets topped up by amounts which have varied widely, because they have been based on the amount of money held back for central services by their former local authorities. According to the Grant Maintained Schools Trust's figures, reported in the *Times Educational Supplement* (15 March 1991) the average top-up this academic year was just over 13 per cent. The Secretary of State for Education Mr. Clarke has announced his decision to raise the top-up budget to 16 per cent. A total amount of £190,000 will be allocated to the GM schools. The average gain by GM schools will be £43,209. In addition GM schools are being allocated grants for major building and refurbishment, and they are also able to bid for capital for major projects. While GM schools are not allowed to have an overdraft, or invest their annual maintenance grant or capital allocation, they are able to build up a pool of money accrued through interest, and they can do what they like with this, even play the stock market.

By September this year (1991), 91 schools will have opted out. The Tories hope to induce more than half of England's schools to have opted out by the end of the next Parliament.

Recent Changes in INSET Funding
Increasing control of INSET has further characterized government policy ostensibly for managerial and accountability purposes. However, INSET is seen by both the Left and the Right as a major and flexible means of effecting educational change whether in the classroom, in the staff room, in the curriculum, in training or in the community. Thus the funding of INSET will always be an important plank in government policy.

Since 1987, the in-service training of teachers has been centrally organized under GRIST and LEATGs. These schemes have followed roughly the same pattern. The Government designates the 'national priorities' for INSET, usually on a yearly basis. LEAs are then obliged to submit in-service plans for approval by the Secretary of State. Plans also, until 1991, included areas of local priority. If the plans were approved, the DES awarded grants of 70 per cent for national priorities and 50 per cent for local priority programmes. The remainder was made up at local level.

INSET provision is also likely to deteriorate through LMS. The average teacher's salary provides the basis for the overall grant to each school, so schools which appoint more experienced (and therefore more expensive) teachers will be forced to offset the expense by reducing other spending such as INSET. Additionally, LEAs will have only limited resources for the provision of supply cover to release teachers for INSET. In the past, 'committed' LEAs have earmarked money though local priority bidding or by allocating lump sums from the education budget. The first avenue is closed and the second increasingly unlikely due to general levels of underfunding.

Through the 1988 Act and other recent changes in education policy, what and how money can be spent has become even more firmly circumscribed and tightly controlled. This is exemplified in the following recent changes in funding.

Grants for Education Support and Training (GEST) is a new objective-driven, tightly prescribed structure of funding combining GRIST, LEATGs and ESG which begins in 1991. Under GEST the local authorities need to find 40 per cent of the money to get a 60 per cent grant from the DES. This change involves removing funding for local INSET priorities in favour of funding only national priorities. Currently, all national priorities are related to the implementation of the National Curriculum. Del Goddard estimates that GEST will result in a real cut of some 6 to 8 per cent in INSET and development work.[7] By removing local priorities, and linking GEST with the policy object, this theoretically has doubled the amount of cash available to the Government to support its initiatives without a single extra penny needing to be found. Goddard argues that GEST is not a grant system related to a total development strategy, to meet the needs of the education service, it is solely concerned with policy implementation and staff development and total Government control of development. Absent from the framework is curriculum and professional development, an understanding of how real improvement takes place and the opportunities for LEAs, schools and colleges to have resources for their own INSET priorities. Consequently, neither those curriculum areas peripheral to the National Curriculum e.g. Drama, nor cross-curricular topics are being funded. Neither can INSET be responsive to local needs. The consequence of this for equal opportunities for example, is that it has all, but disappeared from the educational agenda: the only equal opportunities issue identified as a national priority area for funding is *FE Activity 20 (91) GEST Training for Ethnic Diversity,* and it should be noted that the amount of money allocated for this is extremely limited (£5,000). The objectives for this category are linked with the provision of ESOL (English Speakers of other Languages) courses and thereby assuring equality of opportunity and access.

There is *no* in-service funding at all for anti-racism, gender or for sexual orientation etc. Given the Government's commitment to Radical Right Ideology it is not surprising that money has been removed for equal opportunities training. The Government have chosen not to heed the demographic changes, and the need to train the entire labour force.

Other funding

Section 11 Funding
Section 11 refers to that section of the Local Government Act of 1966 that empowers the Home Secretary to make payments to local authorities 'who in his (sic) opinion are required to make special provision in the exercise of any of their functions in consequence of the presence within their areas of substantial numbers of immigrants from the Commonwealth whose languages or customs differ from those of the community'. It has been argued that S11 represents an anachronistic form of provision when compared with other trends and developments in multi-racial and race relations policy. Nevertheless it has been used 'creatively' by many authorities as a means of both directing extra staff into hard pressed inner-city schools and developing and promoting LEA policy and whole school anti-racist and multi-cultural education.

Under Section 11, LEAs could apply to the Home Office for 75 per cent of the costs of employing extra staff in areas with large numbers of Commonwealth immigrants - for which special provision was perceived as being required because of differences in language and custom. In 1985/6, it was estimated that £71 million of Section 11 money was allocated.

Section 11 has also been reformulated so that it can be used only for staff, appointed on short-term contracts. In the case of education, staff need to work directly with pupils from the New Commonwealth (sic). Section 11 staff cannot spend time engaging in INSET. Moreover, funding is not automatic. Proposals for funding are required to set easily identified targets and devise appropriate evaluation procedures over limited periods of time. Thus, such schemes are unlikely to be able to encourage the long-term changes in professional practice necessary for the introduction of genuinely multi-racial and equality orientated approaches to schooling. Moreover, the revamped Section 11:

a) is being increasingly narrowly targetted. It cannot be used to promote equal opportunities or race equality which, the Government maintains, should be dealt with through ordinary LEA funding. Also, the imposed cash limits are likely to lead to the prioritization or ranking of individual schemes - formerly, funding was automatically allocated on a 75 per cent: 25 per cent central/local government split. Formerly,

Section 11 money could be used for INSET: this has now been curtailed. Work will need to be school-based to qualify for grant and whenever possible should be in the mainstream classroom.

b) stresses the learning of Standard English, rather than, for example, drawing on the strengths of bi-lingual children. Thus, for pre-school children, priority will normally be given to work aimed at enabling young children to acquire English Language competence. It also aims to persuade parents to become involved with the scheme rather than drawing on parents and the local community for advice and support. Thus the schools will be required to set out a school-based plan for establishing contact with parents. This could include regular visits to the home, schemes to involve parents in the child's work and/or arrangements for encouraging parents to come to the school.

c) Focuses on enabling, through instruction, ethnic minority pupils to keep up with peers i.e. to help school-age children from ethnic minorities to achieve at the same level as their peers in all areas of the curriculum and, thus, continues to foster perceptions of black and ethnic minority children as deficient and remedial. Certainly, it fails to recognise the role of sexism/racism/classism in underachievement or the importance of teacher empowerment and increased professionalism in achieving positive educational results. Indeed the Government will not fund programmes aimed at raising achievement generally through multi-cultural approaches.

Training and Enterprise Council (TECs)

Training and Enterprise Councils were first proposed in the Government White Paper, *Employment for the 1990s*, as a way of giving control over training back to employers, 'where it belongs'. Since that time 82 TECs have been set up in England and Wales and 22 Local Enterprise Councils in Scotland.

The Councils are self-appointed bodies but two-thirds of their members must be drawn from senior personnel in local companies. They work under contract to the Department of Employment, which funds them, to fulfil various responsibilities which include existing training provision, such as Youth Training (YT), Employment Training (ET) and Education-Business Partnerships (EBPs) and various initiatives to stimulate local enterprise. They will have guaranteed representation on college governing bodies and on the new Regional Advisory Councils which will responsible for advising the new FE funding council if the proposals in the White Paper (1991), *Employment and Training for the 21st Century,* are enacted. Their involvement in the planning of further education has also been enhanced by the Government's decision to give them control over the 25 per cent of non-advanced FE funding, formerly controlled by the Training Agency.

It is hard to predict what impact, if any, these new bodies will have. The Government clearly intends them to bring about a transformation in cultural attitudes towards training and hence to rectify Britain's renowned skills deficit. They may certainly have some beneficial results in bringing industry more closely in touch with education and encouraging some firms to think more clearly about their training priorities. However, they are unlikely to achieve the kind of revolution in training which the Government intends.

The concept of the TECs comes from the USA like so many government educational ideas. However, they may prove to be a misconstrued borrowing. The US Private Industry Councils were never charged with organizing, let alone transforming, the national training effort in the USA. Their brief was solely concerned with training the long-term unemployed and they have not been very successful at that. It is very unlikely that in the UK such bodies will make any profound impact because they are reliant on employers, the very group which has failed in training so often in the past. The idea of employer-led training is fatally flawed from the start because it ignores the necessity of planning for meeting long-term training needs which are rarely reflected in short-term business thinking. Since the councils are run by directors drawn from a small number of local concerns the chances are that their priorities will reflect the immediate needs of those companies and not the training needs of the communities in which they are based or indeed the long-term needs of industry generally. Nor have they any powers to make companies provide training since the Government has explicitly ruled out any statutory requirements on firms to provide training.

The TECs have wide-ranging powers, and these will be enhanced if the White Paper measures are enacted, and yet they are disturbingly unrepresentative of the groups which have legitimate interests in the planning of training. There is no guarantee that women or minorities are represented on the councils, nor that LEAs or teachers are represented. As such they will always be in danger of becoming self-serving cliques, yet another example of the domination of British education and training by private interest groups.

The White Paper and the Funding of Colleges

New proposals in the White Paper (1991), *Education and Training for the 21st Century*, will, if enacted, alter radically the way sixth-form and further education colleges are funded. Legislation is planned to remove colleges from LEA control and to fund them centrally through new Further Education Funding Councils. These councils, one for England and one for Wales, would consist of 12-15 members directly appointed by the relevant Secretaries of State with a high proportion drawn from industry and commerce. The English Council would be supported by 7 to 10 Regional Advisory Councils, similarly appointed, which would advise it on regional needs and circumstances.

The new funded councils will take over the LEA responsibility for ensuring adequate post-16 provision, will allocate funds to the various colleges and will advise the Secretary of State where necessary on the creation of new colleges and the merger or closure of existing ones. They will be given the power to determine the 'general nature' of a college but it seems unlikely that they will exercise a hands-on approach to planning the sector since the government has said it would prefer market competition to operate with the council simply directing funds to the institutions on the basis of their recruitment and efficiency.

Cash allocations to colleges will be determined on the basis of historic and expected student numbers, weighted to reflect real costs for different courses, but these decisions will be 'informed by quality judgements', and there will be a new mechanism to ensure that funding is adjusted during the year to reflect actual enrolments during that year. There may also be a portion of the funding which is subject to competitive bids from different institutions.

The model for the new FEFC is clearly the PCFC, whose work in funding the polytechnics the Government has much admired. However, there must be some doubt as to whether a system designed for funding some 35 large and essentially national institutions is appropriate for the 510 odd colleges which will come under the control of the FEFC and whose recruitment is local and regional.

Suggestions for new forms of education funding

We suggest that the following funding strategies should be adopted to raise standards in the future:

1. The proportion of total government spending on education should rise.

2. Joint funding of education should continue, but with a higher financial input from central Government. LEAs should be allowed to raise funds at local level as and when democratically decided.

3. Funding of INSET should follow the GRIST and LEATGs patterns with funding for national and local priorities. This encourages INSET planning and accountability from the local provider. Priorities should include promoting greater social and educational equality through the development of anti-sexist, anti-racist, anti-homophobic INSET.

4. A minimum as well as a maximum for LEA spending on education should be set annually so that traditionally low spending authorities can be brought into line in order to equalize educational provision.

5. Adult Education and Skills Training should not be funded out of the same budget and should be recognised as having different functions. Nevertheless, both should be funded at a higher level than at present and both should draw on community needs and national priorities.

6. Section 11 funding should be abolished together with its focus on perceived deficiencies in black and ethnic minority pupils. It should be replaced by the incorporation of multi-racial and equal opportunities perspectives throughout the education service with appropriate funds to support developments at all funding levels, in particular, Teacher Education and INSET.

7. Teachers' salaries should be removed from LMS. Adjustment to the formula should allow for a policy of differential resourcing in order to distribute resources more equitably between the rich and poor part of a local authority.

Appendix

The calculation of Standard Spending Assessment

An SSA will be calculated annually for each authority. SSAs are built up from separate elements for the following major service blocks, and sub-blocks.

I Education
    (i) primary (the number of pupils aged 5-10,
      11-15, 16+)
    (ii) secondary
    (iii) post -16
    (iv) under 5s
    (v) other

II Personal Social Services
    (i) children
    (ii) elderly
    (iii) other

III Police
IV Fire and Civil Defence
V Highway Maintenance
VI All other services
VII Capital Financing

It is the total SSA for an authority which is used for distributing Revenue Support Grant. Local authorities, however, retain discretion over their expenditure priorities between and within services.

The percentages for 1991 to 1992 are as follows:

1.	Education	48.15 %
2.	Personal Social Services	12.41 %
3.	Police	6.58 %
4.	Fire & Civil Defence	2.87 %
5.	Highway Maintenance	5.02 %
6.	All other services	16.67 %
7.	Capital Financing	8.29 %

Taken from a DoE paper *Standard Spending Assessments: Background and underlying methodology.* DoE 1990

Figure 1

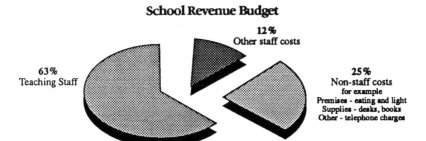

School Revenue Budget

12%
Other staff costs

63%
Teaching Staff

25%
Non-staff costs
for example
Premises - eating and light
Supplies - desks, books
Other - telephone charges

Figure 2

Financing Local Government: The Changes

The old system before April 1990	*The new system from April 1990*
Grants from Central Government (central grant is rate supported)	Grants from Central Government
+	+
Business Rates (raised locally spent locally)	National and Non-Domestic Rates (NNDR) raised locally, pooled nationally, redistributed by central government to local government
+	+
Domestic Rates	Poll Tax
+	+
Income from Local Authority rents, fees, and charges	Income from Local Authority rents, fees, and charges
Local Authority Income	Local Authority Income

Combined effect of the changes
Administrative and organizational chaos in local government already reeling from the impact of a combination of major legislative changes.

Financial loss to inner London (after transitional arrangements) estimated at £1,000 million.

Central government will directly control grants and the NNDR and will have more indirect control over the poll tax and income from local authority rents, fees and charges.
Downward pressure on local authority expenditure.

Notes

1. See Stephen Ball, *Markets, Morality and Equality in Education*, Hillcole Group Paper 5, London: the Tufnell Press, 1990.
2. Coopers and Lybrand, *Local Management of Schools*. A Report to the Department of Education and Science by Coopers and Lybrand, London: HMSO, 1988.
3. Phillip Brown and Hugh Lauder, 'Education, Economy and Society: an Introduction to a New Agenda'. in *Education for Economic Survival: From Fordism to Post-Fordism?*, London: Routledge, 1991, p.9.
4. June Statham, Donald Mackinnon and Heather Cathcart, *The Education Fact File: A Handbook of Education Information in the UK*, London: Hodder and Stoughton, 1989.
5. ibid.
6. DES Press Release 390/90, 11 December 1990.
7. Del Goddard, 'INSET in the 1990s', *Management in Education*, Vol. 4, No. 4, Winter 1990, pp.23-24.

Chapter Eight

A New Education Act

The Hillcole Group

This chapter sets out our various proposals in the form of a new Education Act. Only the main powers, rights and duties of individuals and designated bodies are included together with, where appropriate, the substance of accompanying circulars. Many changes proposed in these papers can be implemented without changes in legislation.

The Act's general aims would be:
To provide for the oversight and development of a public education and training service for the next three decades, serving all citizens throughout their lives;
To raise standards of participation, achievement and provision at all stages of education and training;
To integrate preparation for work with education for personal and community development;
To further a democratically controlled and accountable education service at all levels;
To apply the principles of equality and non-discrimination to all parts of the service;
To contribute to a modernized economy that is committed to protecting the environment and to improving living standards locally, nationally and internationally;
A new Department of Education and Training would be created (DET), replacing the current Departments of Education and Science and of Employment.

From Birth to Compulsory Education
Parents to have rights to have their children admitted to named local care and education facilities - starting with the age range three to five years, within three years from the start of the implementation of reorganization

plans (see below). Facilities for the age range three months to three years would also be included in the plans, and developed concurrently.

Local Education Authorities (LEAs) to be given a duty to survey their existing provision of nursery education, nursery care, childminding, playgroups and creche facilities; to consult locally about the variety of needs for pre-five care and education likely to exist in the next three decades; and, within a year, to prepare plans to reorganize existing provision into a unified service, setting out the expansion required to meet the various needs identified and the stages by which expansion would proceed.

The Secretary of State (by means of a circular) to provide guidance about the type of plans acceptable - and the way they are to be submitted.

Powers to be given to LEAs to develop new provision (including that undertaken in co-operation with voluntary and private providers) subject to approval by the Secretary of State - to be granted only where provision is non-discriminatory and open to all users on an equal basis.

Plans to be forwarded to the Secretary of State within one year.

The Secretary of State to be given the power, where LEAs default on their duty, to send in his/her own representatives - assisted by the appropriate inspectorate - to prepare plans according to the requirements of the Act, working in co-operation with those in the LEA who wish to assist.

The Secretary of State to be given the power to require LEAS to implement plans that have been prepared and approved, and to order such additional provision (e.g. training of staff) as may be required to ensure that there are the variety and numbers of places required to meet local needs and legal obligations to parents and others.

LEAs to be required to review provision regularly and to adjust plans as required to meet local needs

Compulsory Schooling from Five to Sixteen

Comprehensive Reorganization

The same planning requirements and conditions for LEAS (as apply under pre-five reorganization) adjusted for age, to apply in respect of the preparation of plans for completing the comprehensive reorganization of compulsory schooling.

All schools to be consulted on their place in the reorganized system. Plans to take account of reorganization before five and after 16. The process to be guided by a circular stating the ways in which systems can be made comprehensive. This would include the ways in which grammar, CTCs, and opted-out schools are to be developed within the local system as schools receiving all attainments. (Sections of previous education acts to be repealed only where they would prevent the operation of these requirements.)

The Secretary of State to provide a further circular giving guidance on the development of out-of-school care on school premises for pupils before school in the morning and after school in the afternoon; LEAs to have the power to develop this provision - in co-operation with Social Services.

LEAs

LEAs to have a duty to maintain the needs of all schools in balance (as the Audit Commission recommends) and to ensure that comparable educational opportunities are available in each. LEAs to consult each school yearly to determine the level of funding appropriate to it in view of its pupil numbers, their particular needs, the state of the school's facilities and fabric, the state of development of its curriculum and assessment, its provision for equal opportunities, the amount of extra-state funding it can rely upon, the area it serves and any other matters the Secretary of State requires the LEAs to take into account.

LEAs to have the duty - within government guidelines, and after consultation with all other schools likely to be affected - to decide the size of schools and the total numbers admitted to each. LEAs also to have certain new powers to assist smaller schools. Open enrolment requirements to be repealed.

LEAs to have a duty to report on the spending of schools in relation to their numbers, PTR, equipment, books, repairs, and financial administration - with powers to order specific development only where pupils' or students' rights to a broad and balanced common curriculum (see below), or to a non-discriminatory education (see below), are being endangered; or where funds are being mispent.

The legal power to hire and dismiss teachers to return to LEAs, who also have the right to be represented at staff appointments.

Schools

Schools to have the power to manage their own budgets and exercise virement within specific areas of expenditure; and to appoint their own staff (subject to LEA guidelines on procedure as legal employers). School governors to hear staff appeals, with reference upward to LEAs only if not resolved at school level.

LMS provisions under existing law to be repealed only to the extent that the duties of LEAs and schools (in the previous sections) would require it.

Competitive tendering requirements would be repealed and schools and colleges left free to organize meals, cleaning, repairs and certain other educational services as they chose - in consultation with their LEAs, who would have the duty to oversee standards and value for money. LEAs to have the power to organize services directly and to invite schools to use them.

As part of their duty to keep the needs of all their schools in balance and to organize admissions giving every child a right to enter a named local school (see below), LEAs to be given the duty to plan for all voluntary schools on the same basis as county schools (separate Diocesan Board planning to cease). Voluntary schools to be consulted individually about their place in the system (and their yearly financial needs) on the same basis as county schools.

The requirement that aided schools pay 15 per cent of their capital costs to be repealed, and both county and voluntary schools to be funded on the same basis.

All governing bodies of schools and colleges to be required to elect at least one representative of their support staff; and all institutions with students over the age of 16 to have at least two students (one male, one female, where appropriate) as full voting governors. The legal requirement to have a representative of business to be repealed. Schools and colleges to co-opt as they wish individually.

All teachers and governors in both county and voluntary schools to have the same legal rights and responsibilities.

Harmonization

A Harmonization Commission to be set up to see through the process of bringing voluntary and county schooling more closely together in governing, funding, admissions and employment practices.

The Harmonization Commission to be required to make recommendations about the use of schools and colleges for worship or instruction in respect of both Christian denominations and the major world religions in areas where these are represented in any significant numbers - on the basis that all religions should be granted equal rights within the system.

Religious Worship and Education

All schools, county and voluntary, to be given the right to choose individually - after consultation with parents, staff and pupils - whether to have secular, mainly Christian, or multi-faith assemblies. The legal requirement for every school to have a daily assembly and for every assembly in every school to be mainly Christian to be repealed.

Religious education to cease to be a special legal requirement, but education in major world faiths to be part of the common curriculum of all schools' humanities education. Any school can add additional religious education to its optional section of the curriculum (see below).

Private Education

The Assisted Places Scheme to be repealed. The governors of assisted schools to be required to consult their bursars and parents, including the parents of assisted pupils, about ways and means of keeping on such pupils as wish to remain. Local authorities to be empowered to help with fees only for a two year period, or up to 16 or 18, whichever comes first.

No LEA or agency of central government, including the DET, to be able to spend public money on any school charging fees (other than places in schools catering wholly for those with disabilities) or in any school or training establishment practicing attainment selection or any other form of discrimination (see below).

The payment of public money for the private school fees of the children of diplomats or military officers or others with overseas assignments to end (such schemes to be discontinued on the same basis as the Assisted Places Scheme). A system of allowances to be instituted to permit children with absent parents to live with relatives or friends and attend state schools in Britain, including new state-funded boarding schools - in those cases where the overseas post has no appropriate education available, and the income of the parents is below a set level.

New conditions for private schools that charge fees to be set out, including a requirement that they meet certain standards (e.g. in health and safety matters), and meet all their own costs, making no charge on public expenditure. Provision would be made in the Act for all such schools to be levied for services they receive from the state and/or the local authority, at set rates: e.g. teachers trained at state expense, HMI inspection, use of teacher exchange facilities and teachers' centres; and certain local recreational facilities.

The law on charities to be revised to remove from charitable status all schools and colleges which fail to provide education or training 'for a range of clear educational needs throughout the whole community' (as recommended by the Goodman Committee on Charity Law, 1976).

Curriculum and Assessment

A National Council for Curriculum, Qualifications and Assessment (CCQA) would be created (to replace in the first instance SEAC and the NCC) with duties to advise and report on the development of curricula and qualifications appropriate to a comprehensive system; to make available a range of tests for use for diagnostic purposes in schools; and to monitor educational progress nationally. A proportion of places to be reserved for representatives from teaching, parent and student organizations and such other groups as may be decided. Wales and Scotland to have their own CCQAs.

The CCQA - advised by HMIs - to have the duty to set out guidelines for devising a common curriculum for schools up to 16 (and core areas after 16) and to advise on the curriculum areas that are optional and what the limits for them would be.

All schools to be required to implement a common curriculum that is broad and balanced and covers the required areas of learning set down by the CCQA. Optional time is for schools to devise individually - provided all options are open to all pupils equally.

All parents to have a right for their children to experience a broad and balanced curriculum, taken in common with all other pupils in any given school up to the age of 16, and any common core of learning laid down thereafter by the CCQA from 16 to 18.

All parents to have the right to have their children assessed regularly in basic literacy and numeracy, and in older years, in the major areas of learning.

The existing National Curriculum would not be a legal requirement in any school but schools that had developed the National Curriculum (as set out under the 1988 Act) and wished to retain it, could do so, provided it also met the requirements of a common curriculum as defined in this Act.

The requirement on schools to consult the police about their curriculum to be repealed. Schools to be free to consult any members of the community on any matter.

The legal requirement for national testing at 7,11,14 and 16 would be repealed and replaced with the development of a wide range of tests made available to schools to choose individually for use for diagnostic purposes, at whatever ages they choose to use them.

Parents of children under 16 would have the right to see all pupil records and to know of all assessments and tests conducted, and their import. The confidentiality of all testing in schools would be protected, as matters for individual pupils and their parents - with the LEAs and DET having access only for general monitoring purposes (see below). Schools to decide individually how they report pupil progress and school performance to parents and the community.

The CCQA would be required to develop a system of Records of Achievement for all pupils in schools, and for students in education and training from 16 through to 18.

The CCQA to be required to conduct national samples of attainment (unrelated to individual schools or LEAs) to monitor national standards of learning and competence in literacy and numeracy and in the major areas of learning experience - languages, English, science, mathematics, the arts and physical education, the humanities, technology education and various skill fields.

14-16
The CCQA - together with the NCVQ and the examining bodies, and assisted by HMI - would be required to develop a unified modular curriculum and assessment system from 14 through 18 to replace in stages all existing qualifications, courses and schemes open to this age group.

Starting first with ages 14-16, the CCQA would help schools progressively to convert GCSE to modular courses each carrying credits, and to assist teachers in developing, and externally moderating, the in-school assessment required. When the new system is in place, external examinations at 16-plus to end.

The Act to set a single leaving date at the end of the summer term of the school year in which the student has reached sixteen and GCSE has been taken.

Admissions
It would be illegal for any school receiving public funds to use attainment or other tests for the purpose of selecting entrants.

Current admissions arrangements to schools to remain - subject to the LEAs' duties to decide numbers (see above) and to the following right for all parents: to have each child admitted to a named local school (and pre-five facility) at each stage of their education. (See accompanying note on 'Choice.')

Choices of other schools to be accommodated on the same basis as at present (with existing rights of appeal retained) and schools required to admit pupils subject to existing provisions (e.g. school not 'full', no extra cost to LEA) except where admission would prevent entry to the school of a pupil already offered it as of right.

LEAs to be given guidance concerning right of entry to certain denominational schools, to ensure as good a match as possible between a wish for education in such a school and available places.

Post-16

National assemblies in Scotland and Wales (with such regional authorities as they designate) and regional authorities in England, would be created to devolve government more effectively. They would be democratically elected. Greater London would be a new region.

The Act to provide for the development and oversight of all education and training after 16 to be the responsibility of the two assemblies (and their regions) and the regional authorities through their Education and Training Committees (RETA).

A single national funding body would allocate money to assemblies and regions for the development of education and training over the age of 16, and the funding of all institutions catering for this age range. Regional Authorities and their RETAs would decide how to allocate funds between their institutions, consulting each one, guided by their post-16 reorganization planning. All post-16 institutions would have the right to make representations related to their needs (for research, see later).

The Act to lay down what additional members should be co-opted to RETAs in addition to elected members - to represent the interests of the voluntary bodies, staff working in educational institutions, women, local groups, trade unions, and employers.

TECs (Training and Enterprise Councils) to be abolished and the funding currently coming to them, to be given to RETAs, who would be accountable for this spending, and for developing and delivering education and training in their regions.

16-19

RETAs to be given the duty to plan for the comprehensive reorganization of education and training from 16 onwards, beginning with 16-19, and with post-18 education to follow on from it. (Submission and planning conditions the same as set down earlier in the Act for pre-five and compulsory sector, adjusted for age range.)

RETAs to be required to consult all existing schools and colleges with students in this age range - with a view to preparing plans for a unified system of education and training under a single set of regulations, and to plan the growth in existing (or new) institutions that would be required to to accommodate, in stages, the entire 16-18 age group, and thereafter, a planned progressive increase in adult numbers.

The Secretary of State to provide a circular showing the forms of 16-19 organization from which choice may be made in order to offer a rational and comprehensive service; to allow for an expansion of numbers; to provide for equal opportunities; and to offer a reasonable choice of courses. An additional circular would be provided after two years to guide on the first stage of post-18 planning and the growth required to accommodate adults (see above and below).

Courses 16-19

The CCQA (see above) to develop all existing qualifications (A Levels, NCVQs, BTEC, CPVE, City and Guilds etc.) within a single new national system of modular courses, carrying credits. Scotland to develop its own SCOTVEC on comparable and compatible lines. The new system to be in place to receive new entrants within three years.

A new single qualification to be developed to be granted at 18 to every student or trainee who has completed the requisite number of 'credits' by study, including training on the job after 16, of modules/courses in the prescribed areas between 14 and 18. (There would be several such areas, each providing a variety of academic and vocational and training modules at basic, intermediate, and advanced levels.)

The CCQA to make recommendations about core modules for 16-19, to be taken by all students.

RETAs to have a duty to develop institutions that can provide the means to gain this qualification for all who wish to attempt it and who reach a basic standard.

Adults of any age to be eligible to join classes to achieve credits in particular courses (or the full award). Post-16 colleges to be open to them on the same basis as for younger students; places on such courses in schools with pupils below the age of 16 to be open to them at the discretion of the school's governors.

Entry

Each person at 16-plus to have the right to enter a named local college for continuation of his or her education. RETAs to have the duty to provide a reorganized local system which makes this possible within three years from the start of approval of their plan (see earlier).

Each adult from age 18 to have the right to call upon a named local college for educational and training advice, and, in time (as expansion continues) the right to attend. Within five years all adults to be given the right to a minimum of one week's education or paid educational leave, increasing over time.

All students to have the right to choose from a comprehensive range of vocational and academic and training modules in order to achieve the national qualification within the requirements of the field where he or she wishes to continue study or apply for work. This range to be comparable with other colleges in the RETA area and with colleges nationally.

Where sufficient numbers of students up to the age of 18 are not of a standard to start a course or module they wish to choose, the RETA will to have a duty to provide access courses.

Information to be provided to assist people to make informed choices.

All students to have the right to see their records and to be given the results of tests and assessments which they have undergone.

Post-18

Decisions about the funding of all post-18 institutions, including all further education colleges, universities and polytechnics in Scotland and Wales to be devolved to Scottish and Welsh national assemblies, who in turn will decide what grants to give their own Regional Authorities and RETAs. Grants from a single national funding body for all post-sixteen education in England to be given in block to the region to decide for itself how to distribute within the guidelines laid down by the Secretary of State, assisted by advice from the appropriate body. The Secretary of State will have the power to give advice, and in exceptional circumstances, to intervene to see that the rights and duties as set out in legislation are upheld, and public funds used correctly.

The Secretary of State to have the power to lay down the minimum number and level of courses which a specific RETA (or college within that authority) should provide, to bring it up to the national standard.

While development plans for post-18 education in each RETA would not be required immediately, the Act would give the Secretary of State the power to require preliminary proposals from all RETAs after a period of two years, and to fix the date for reorganization of the post-18 sector to begin at any time onwards from a date not more than two years after their 16-19 reorganization plans have been approved.

At that time RETAs to have the duty (in co-operation with sectoral bodies and professional associations) to prepare plans to show how they would provide courses and options in both education and training throughout the adult age group that match the numbers wishing to study or train (or retrain), that meet the needs of local industries and services, and that allow for diversity of options to be exercised.

After 18, RETAs would have the power to provide access courses in all areas of learning (and the power to apply for grants to assist institutions developing them - see below). They would also have the power to develop literacy and numeracy learning in any institution.

All institutions with students over 18 to have the power to validate degree-level work carrying credits (and in certain cases to grant degrees) subject to the approval of the Secretary of State and the advice of the appropriate national body.

The Act to make provision under certain conditions for courses to be initiated at the request of groups of citizens - with schools or colleges providing validation, instruction and assessment - where approved by the LA or RETA and the Secretary of State.

Education and Training

RETAs would have the power to create and finance special working parties to develop education and training in any part of its area, relating to the needs of the community (locally, nationally, and internationally) as well as to the needs of employers and employees. Such committees would operate in co-operation with national sectoral and professional bodies and the local Careers Service.

No employer should be legally allowed to employ anyone between the ages of 16 and 19 for more than 20 hours a week, without making arrangements to release them for education and training. Those employing under 20 hours would have to provide/or arrange for provision of basic 'common core' education as required by the CCQA.

All people on courses or at work would have the right to join a union during training; to be released from work for education and training up to 18, and after 18, to apply for release and, if refused, to have reasons given, with a right to appeal.

Wages for work done while training (at whatever age) should be negotiated by the appropriate trade union, generally at the 'rate for the job'. Trainees receiving wages would not receive basic student income (see below).

No public funding for training in any firm to be authorized (or consortia membership approved) where trade unions are prohibited or where trainees or employees experience any obstruction in organizing in unions at the workplace.

Provision for a legal requirement for all employers to pay 1 per cent of payroll as their contribution to the development of a national education and training programme. Larger companies which are already spending this on their own training programmes to be exempt provided their programmes involve training for the industry or sector, not just for their own needs.

All firms, whatever their size, to be required by law to prepare training and education plans for their employees - in consultation with workplace committees. Such committees to be established in each firm, or by RETAs for smaller firms in consortia.

Sectoral bodies to be created to complete the cover of all major areas of industry and services, and to plan the education and training each requires. These to be linked with the bodies that oversee entry into the professions. A group drawn from both sides to be set up to monitor the long-term needs for skilled and professional personnel.

Entry into all work, both skilled and professional, to be organized in a unified system by the Careers Service and developed nationally under unified regulations.

The Careers Service to be given new duties, including overseeing, in co-operation with RETAs, the entry to training of all young people from 16 through to 22 (or through to first employment). The Careers Service to have powers to require from employers information about the way jobs are filled, and to make recommendations to the the RETA or the Secretary of State about access and equal opportunities.

Teacher Education

Provision to be made to establish a) two-year teacher education courses as an additional route to qualification, b) certification of teacher assistants and c) access courses for intending teachers. A core curriculum to be prepared for all teachers in training; and in-service education for all teachers for stated periods to be guaranteed.

Ear Marked Grants

While funding generally is by block grants to RETAs or to LEAS, additional grants could also be made by the Secretary of State directly to RETAS or LEAS or to institutions individually or severally, for specific purposes, encouraging developments over and above those the Act requires.They would be bid for, and implementation optional.

Among them might be grants

to encourage diversification of provision in institutions (e.g. access courses for adults in higher education, degree-level courses for credits in further education)

to encourage the conduct of research in FE colleges

to develop academic, vocational and training courses in off-site venues (workplaces, community centres, public libraries, etc.)

to develop independent learning systems, including the use of cable system TV

to develop schemes teaching the elderly, the disabled or those with young children in their own homes

to develop equality programmes dealing with race, gender, age, sexuality, class and disability

to help schools that wish to unstream classes (with inset training) or to develop new pedagogical approaches that enhance the effectiveness of comprehensive education

to encourage schools and colleges to remain open in the evenings, at weekends, and in holidays, for educational, recreational, cultural and training purposes

Research

National research councils to continue to receive funding and to award grants for research. A new council to be added that provides funding in the field of the humanities. The Social Sciences Council to include research in the field of education and training. Anyone would be eligible to put forward proposals for research, including all educational institutions and groups of individuals.

Further Provisions

Corporal punishment to continue to be illegal in all schools and colleges, and to be made illegal in all pre-five care and education. Other forms of punishment or control to be monitored by HMIs.

A national unit to be established within the DET to monitor equality within the system, with power to require from RETAs and LEAs reports of their own local monitoring in specific areas of practice, intake, provision, achievement, take-up and outcome, with regard to gender, class, income, disability, age, religion, and race.

Clause 28 of the 1988 Local Government ACT to be repealed and replaced with a new clause making it unlawful in the provision or conduct of education or training at any level, for any group or individual, by virtue of age, race, religion, gender, sexual orientation, class, or disability, to be discriminated against.

A new national *Advisory Council* to be created to conduct wide ranging enquiries into education and training, and to guide the task of national development. One area to be reported upon to be the organization, funding, admissions, and arrangements for expenditure of public monies in the colleges of Oxford and Cambridge; with recommendations for making the advantages of these institutions more widely available to the local and national community.

All schools, colleges and training establishments to be required to hold democratic assemblies at least twice a year, open to all pupils and students over 13 and all staff (and to parents also in compulsory or pre-school education) where issues of general concern to the institution, its users and the community it serves, can be raised and discussed. Such assemblies to be able to elect their own officers and make their own recommendations. Governors to be required to take its representations into account.

Other Legislation

The Social Security laws to be overhauled in order to guarantee everyone the means to survive and live when not (or unable to be) employed.

One of its sections should relate to students from 16 through adult life and should provide a basic income for those who are bona fide students full time (pro rata part-time) and are without parental, partner or other financial support. The level of basic support will not be related to the level of the course undertaken but to the needs of the student and the other income he or she can rely upon. This income is to replace a system of grants and allowances from LEA/RETAs (and would be pegged at a level always higher than unemployment allowances). The purpose is to encourage as many people as possible to continue education and training and to offer basic support for those who choose to continue.

No post-18 institution should be able to charge fees to any full-time student on basic student-income. Other students could be charged according to means up to a level that would be set by the Secretary of State, with the advice of the appropriate national body. Any student whose parents paid fees between 16 and 18 would be assumed to be able to continue to pay at the highest level unless he or she could demonstrate otherwise.

A new Housing Act to have a requirement to provide grants to LEAs and RETAs and local Housing Committees for the accommodation of students attending colleges, schools and universities in each area - in cooperation with the educational establishments concerned. The basic standards of accommodation would be the same for all students, regardless of course attended. Institutions to share accommodation.

A new Employment Act to set out equal training and employment rights for all adults over 18. An explanatory note, giving more detail about one objective of a new Education Act: to make as many choices as possible equally available to everyone.

Choice

Equality does not require everyone to be alike - or choose 'the same'- but in a public education service it should require equal rights to experience common education during compulsory years and an equal chance to choose from the same range of alternatives before and after this time.

In much present practice the word 'choice' is misused as a cover for the exercise of privilege, the 'choice' in question being open only to a minority.

To redefine choice as a right which everyone can exercise - should be the objective of an education system determined to develop greater social justice as well as to encourage as many as possible to participate in education and training.

Rights

In general, we should thus redirect the idea of choice (and funding of education) more to courses of education than to institutions.

At the same time, there are important policy aspects of admissions we should address with regard to institutional access.

New policy should aim to make entry at all stages relate to the communities served, however large or small. Every neighbourhood should have a school and every community a college, each of which is able to offer the full range of courses generally available for the age ranges they accept (comprehensive in the basic meaning of this term). For the post-18 institutions of national and international reputation, it should include a requirement to extend educational commitment to the immediate and local (commuting) community - with percentages allocated for development in relation to eligibility for funding.

Policy should encourage schools and colleges to identify with, and serve, their own communities - as positive ways of developing those communities. This means moving away from the exclusive pre-occupation with running institutions as competing businesses, divorced from those communities except for certain employer concerns. Efficiency is essential but it is not the only purpose of education; nor are employers the only members of the community.

Right of Entry

This would be a new principle.

Never in British education (as in the case in many other countries) has any parent or pupil - or in later years, any student or adult person - ever had any legal right to attend any school or college, even if the institution was next door.

In future, every parent of a school child (and in time every parent of a child three or over), and after 16, all young people up to 18, should have offered to them a named local school (or nursery facility) or college where their child/they may attend *as of right.* In time, this right would extend beyond 18. Initially, however, the rights beyond 18 would be limited to specific short periods, and to a right to receive information or counselling about opportunities that are available.

For those with rights in schools and colleges, it would mean that the local and regional authorities would have a duty to draw catchment boundaries or arrange links with lower schools, in order to provide entry as of right to everyone likely to exercise their rights to education, and situated conveniently for parents and students. And to review these arrangements regularly to take account of demographic changes.

Parents/students would get a *named* school or college where their children/students have a place which would be retained for them unless they give notice they do not wish to take it up.

For those parents or students who wish to be considered for another school or college, the existing legal right to choose any other school or college should be retained - along with the legal requirement on the school or college chosen to accept such pupils/students (subject to restrictions already applying about cost, room in the school, etc.) so long as acceptance will not displace any pupil/student whose 'named' school or college' it is.

To make this work, comprehensive reorganization is necessary. For all institutions should offer a full range of courses appropriate to the age groups they contain. At compulsory level most already do. Those few that do not would be required to develop further by the LEA as it completes any outstanding comprehensive reorganization.

Post-16

Every institution (or consortia) with the 16-19 age range would be required to have available a comparable range of courses (academic, vocational and training). A minimum requirement would be laid down to provide for some 80 per cent or 90 per cent of all likely choices.

Where it is a case of provision of specialist or unusual courses, their planning in specific locations should be overseen by regional education authorities (in co-operation with the colleges) so that the distribution throughout the area is rational.

It should be possible for students based in their 'home' college to travel to others for specialist courses, as well as to employers' or other premises for work, training or education. The reorganization of post-16 education would mean in any case that some new institutions would occupy several sites.

Course Choice

During compulsory education choice would be exercised within the optional areas of each school's common curriculum. All options should be open to all pupils to choose ; no 'choices' open only to the 'bright' or the 'less academic'; and no heavy guidance to enforce choice that is convenient for the institutions.

During the final two years of compulsory schooling, all young people should have made known to them the full range of courses and training opportunities available in the area's post-16 colleges, including the college that is theirs to attend by right - as well as the arrangements for entering local employment that apply in the area.

Although counselling is helpful in explaining the choices, no student should be 'directed' to any path.

Whatever the student's choice of education and training - whether full or part-time or declined for the time being - all young people at 16 would be attached to a named college (or to the Careers Service) and their progress overseen by the LEA/RETA. It should be a legal duty on the authority to keep track of every young person up to 18 and to keep those who have dropped out informed of the choices that are still open to them, and will remain open to them.

After 18

The principle that should govern education and training for this age group in future is that they choose to learn or train - not whether they are 'qualified' to do so.

At 18 young people could remain attached to their colleges if they wished to continue study and it offered the education or training they wished to take, or they could choose to attend another college.

The LEA/RETA and the Careers Service should be required to keep available, and to provide information about, the full range of courses and training available in the area to everyone over 18 who asks for it. This should include all university and higher education colleges in the area (as well as elsewhere) and all professional training as well as all FE and adult education, and craft/skill training.

Where courses require pre-entry qualifications, the information should show clearly how these may be obtained in the area. Where such access or pre-entry courses are not available, local and regional authorities should have the duty - in certain circumstances - to see they are provided.

The objective is for each regional area to make sure that each of its institutions is able to provide (alone or in consortia) the full range of study and training (the latter related as required to the industries and trades of the area) normally available for adults and to provide access to all the main academic and vocational 'pathways'.

Those areas unable to provide a full range would be helped to do so as a priority. So that as soon as possible every region offers a comparable choice. This would include pre-5 education as well as post-5, post-16, and post-18 to the end of life. It would not be accomplished quickly, but planning should show clearly the stages by which it would be achieved.

To encourage as many students and trainees as possible to undertake their initial post-16 and post-18 education, and their continuing education and training, including degree level work, within their own areas or regions (where they can live at home and so reduce education's costs), all institutions offering post-18 education should be required in future to maintain a minimum percentage of their intake from their own commuting community or region as a condition of retaining full funding.

Those who wish to choose outside their own areas (and to live elsewhere) would be able to do so in the same way as they can now. It would cost more, however. Who should bear that extra cost is a matter for further debate. It could be that once each region can provide a comparable service, that living costs for those opting in from outside become a charge colleges have to pay themselves (and budget for). In general, it should not be students who have to pay more for exercising their choice.

Along with these policies would go an enhanced development of the Open University and an expansion of public programmes of independent learning - both essential to extend choice.

Initiatives for studying or training should not be left to official institutions/authorities to devise and 'sell', but should be encouraged to come from individuals, groups and communities themselves. There should be scope for people over 18 at any time of life, to choose to study what interests them, or what they need to know for personal or collective development, and to have the help of local colleges/ authorities in devising courses of learning or training that meet their needs. The progressive development of this provision would be a key element in extending choice in education and training.

Bibliography

Alcock, P. 'Why Citizenship and Welfare Rights Offer New Hope for New Welfare in Britain' *Critical Social Policy*, Issue 26, Autumn, 1989.

AUT, *Goodwill Under Stress*, 1990.

AUT, *Widening Opportunities*, 1982.

Baker, J. *Arguing for Equality*, London: Verso, 1987.

Ball, S. *Markets, Morality and Equality in Education*, Hillcole Group Paper 5, London: the Tufnell Press, 1990.

Benn, C. 'The Public Price of Private Education and Privatization'. *Forum*, Vol. 32, No. 3, Summer 1990, pp.68-73.

Benn, C. *All Faiths in All Schools*, SEA, 1986.

Bishop, A.S., *The Rise of a Central Authority for English Education*, Cambridge University Press, 1971, p.vii.

Booth, M., Furlong, J., and Wilkin, M. *Partnership in Initial Teacher Training*, London: Cassell, 1990.

Brown, P. and Lauder, H., 'Education, Economy and Society: An Introduction to a new Agenda' in Brown, P. and Lauder, H. (eds.) *Education for Economic Survival: From Fordism to Post-Fordism?*, London: Routledge, 1991.

Brundtland Report *Our Common Future, World Commission on Environment and Development*, Oxford: Oxford University Press 1987.

Chitty, C. *Towards a New Education System: the Victory of the New Right?* Lewes: Falmer Press, 1989.

Chitty, C (ed.) *Post-Sixteen Education: Studies in Access and Achievement*, London: Kogan Page, 1991.

Clay, J., Cole, M., and Hill, D. 'Black Achievement in Initial Teacher Education - How do we Proceed into the 1990s,' *Multicultural Teaching*, Vol. 8, No. 3, Summer 1990.

Cole, M., Clay, J., and Hill, D. 'The Citizen as 'individual' and nationalist or as 'social' and internationalist? What is the role of education?' *Critical Social Policy*, Vol. 10, No. 3, 1991.

Coopers and Lybrand, *Local Management of Schools*. A Report to the Department of Education and Science, by Coopers and Lybrand, London: HMSO, 1988.

Croft, S. and Beresford, P. 'User-Involvement, Citizenship and Social Policy' *Critical Social Policy*, Issue 26, Autumn, 1989.

Department of Education and Science (DES), *Education and Training for the 21st Century*, London: HMSO, Cmnd. 1536, May 1991.

Department of the Environment, (DoE), *Standard Spending Assessments: Background and Underlying Methodology*, London: Department of the Environment, 1990.

Deucher, S. *History and GCSE History*, London: Centre for Policy Studies, 1987.

Goddard, D. 'INSET in the 1990s', *Management in Education*, Vol. 4, No. 4, Winter, 1990, pp.23-24.

Graves, N. (ed.) *Initial Teacher Education: Policies and Progress*, London: Kogan Page, 1990.

Green Party, *Green Party Policy- Education* and *Green Party Education Working Group: Education*, both undated but sent to enquirers in 1990; and *Manifesto for a Sustainable society*, 1990.

Hill, D. *Charge of the Right Brigade*, Hillcole Group/Institute for Education Policy Studies, 1989.

Hill, D. *What's Left in Teacher Education: Teacher Education, The Radical Left and Policy Proposals*, Hillcole Group Paper 6, London: the Tufnell Press, 1991.

Hiskett, M. *Choice in Rotten Apples: Bias in GCSE Examining Groups*, Centre for Policy Studies, 1988.

Hutton, W. 'Why our choice -based education system is developing into one of the world's most sophisticated forms of social apartheid', *The Guardian*, 14 January 1991.

Institute for Public Policy Research (IPPR) *A British Baccalauréat: ending the division between education and training*, IPPR, 1990.

Jones, K. *Right Turn: The Conservative Revolution in Education*, London: Hutchinson Radius, 1989.

Labour Party, *16-19: Learning for Life*, The Labour Party, 1982

Labour Policy Review, *Meet the Challenge. Make the Change*, The Labour Party 1989.

Maclure, S. *Educational Documents: England and Wales: 1816 to the present day*, London: Methuen, 1986.

National Union of Teachers (NUT), *A Strategy for the Curriculum*, London: NUT, 1990.

O'Hear, A. 'Black Marks for CGSE' in *The Times Educational Supplement*, 6 October 1989.

O'Hear, A. 'The GCSE Philosophy of Education,' in North, J. (ed.) *The GCSE: An Examination*, London: the Claridge Press, 1987.

Plaid Cymru, *Wales in Europe* and *Programme for the 90s*, both 1990.

Lynn, R. Educational *Achievement in Japan*, London: Macmillan, 1988.

Scruton, R. *The Meaning of Conservatism*, London: Macmillan, 1980.

Scruton, R., Ellis Jones, A. and O'Keefe, D. (eds.) *Education and Indoctrination*, Education Research Centre, 1985.

Sexton, S. *Our Schools - A Radical Policy*, The Institute of Economic Affairs, 1987.

Simon, B. 'Thatcher's Third Tier, or Bribery and Corruption,' *Forum*, Vol. 32, No. 3, Summer, 1990, pp.74-78.

SLD, *Putting Pupils First*, No 3 Federal Paper; *Higher Education, Investing in Our Future*, No 14, 1990, *The Learning Society*, No. 5, 1990

SNP, *Policy Summary No 1* and *SNP Priorities for Scottish Education*, both 1990.

Socialist Party of Great Britain, *Socalist Standard*, October, 1989.

Statham, J., Mackinnon, D. and Cathcart, H. *The Education Fact File: A Handbook of Education Information in the UK*, London: Hodder and Stoughton, 1989.

The National Labour Movement Inquiry into Education, Training and Unemployment, Birmingham Trade Union Resources Center, 1987.

TUC, *Childcare and Nursery Education*, 1989.

Turner, B.S. *Equality*, Chichester and London: Horwood (Ellis) Ltd and Tavistock, 1986.

Wale, W. and Irons, E.J. 'An Evaluative Study of Texas Alternative Certification Programs.' Paper presented at the Annual Meeting of the American Educational Research Association, Boston, Mass. 1990.

Glossary of Acronyms

ACET	Advanced Certificate of Education and Training
AERA	American Educational Research Association
AMB	Area Management Board
APEL	Alternative Prior Experience and Learning
AUT	Association of University Teachers
BERA	British Educational Research Association
BTEC	Business and Technician Education Council
CARE	Campaign for Anti-Racist Education
CATE	Committee for the Accreditation of Teacher Education
CBI	Confederation of British Industry
CEA	Council for Educational Advance
CPS	Centre for Policy Studies
CPVE	Certificate of Pre-Vocational Education
CTC	City Technology College
DES	Department of Education and Science
DHSS	Department of Health and Social Security
DoE	Department of the Environment
DoH	Department of Health
DSS	Department of Social Security
EEC/EC	European Economic Community
EIS	Educational Institute of Scotland
EMA	Education Maintenance Allowance
ESL	English as a Second Language
ESS	Education Support Group
EWO	Education Welfare Officer
FE	Further Education
FEFC	Further Education Funding Council
GCET	General Certificate of Education and Training
GCSE	General Certificate of Secondary Education
GDP	Gross Domestic Product
GEST	Grant for Education Support and Training
GLC	Greater London Council
GMS	Grant Maintained School/Grant Maintained Status
GRE	Grant Related Entitlement
GRIST	Grant Related In-service Training
HE	Higher Education
HMI	Her Majesty's Inspectorate
ILEA	Inner London Education Authority
ILP	Independent Labour Party
INSET	In-service Training
IPPR	Institute of Public Policy Research
ITE	Initial Teacher Education

JTS   Job Training Scheme
LEA   Local Education Authority
LEATG   Local Education Authority Training Grant
LMS   Local Management of Schools
MSC   Manpower Services Commission
NAS/UWT National Association of Schoolmasters/Union of Women Teachers
NATFHE National Association of Teachers in Further and Higher Education
NCC   National Curriculum Council
NCVQ   National Council for Vocational Qualifications
NEC   National Executive Committee
NLM   National Labour Movement
NUT   National Union of Teachers
NVQ   National Vocational Qualification
PCFC   Polytechnics and Colleges Funding Council
PEL   Paid Education Leave
PGCE   Post Graduate Certificate of Education
PTR   Pupil Teacher Ratio
QTS   Qualified Teacher Status
SAT   Standard Assessment Task
SDP   Social Democrat Party
SEA   Socialist Education Association
SEAC   Schools Examination and Assessment Council
SLD   Social and Liberal Democrats
SNP   Scottish Nationalist Party
TANEA   Towards a New Education Act
TEC   Training and Enterprise Council
TGAT   Task Group on Assessment and Testing
TUC   Trades Union Congress
TVEI   Technical and Vocational Education Initiative
UCET   University Council for the Education of Teachers
WEA   Workers Education Association
YCL   Youth Communist League
YTS   Youth Training Scheme